MW00777019

HARD BOP
Academy

THE SIDEMEN OF ART BLAKEY AND THE JAZZ MESSENGERS

Alan Goldsher

HAL•LEONARD®

Published by Hal Leonard Corporation
7777 West Bluemound Road
P.O. Box 13819
Milwaukee, WI 53213, USA

Trade Book Division Editorial Offices:
151 West 46th Street, 8th Floor
New York, NY 10036

Visit Hal Leonard online at **www.halleonard.com**

Library of Congress Cataloging-in-Publication Data

Goldsher, Alan, 1966-
  Hard bop academy : the sidemen of Art Blakey and the Jazz Messengers /
Alan Goldsher.-- 1st ed.
      p. cm.
Includes bibliographical references.
  ISBN 0-634-03793-5
  1. Jazz musicians. 2. Blakey, Art, 1919- 3. Jazz Messengers. I.
Title.
  ML395 .G63 2002
  781.65'5--dc21
                                        2002014826

Printed in the United States of America
First Edition

10 9 8 7 6 5 4 3 2 1

TABLE OF CONTENTS

Acknowledgments

I'D INITIALLY envisioned this book as a small, personal project, a love letter to Art Blakey and the Jazz Messengers. I'd hoped that a few graduates of the Hard Bop Academy would come along for the ride, but I had no idea that so many musicians were not just willing but eager to share their thoughts, their memories, and their adoration of Buhaina.

A true Jazz Messenger through and through, Javon Jackson was an essential part in the construction of *Hard Bop Academy*. His infectious enthusiasm, his accessibility, his kindness, and his phat Rolodex helped give voice (and voices) to this project. I'm not exaggerating when I say that this book wouldn't have been half the book it is if it hadn't been for Javon.

Bobby Watson, Branford Marsalis, and Terence Blanchard—three of the busiest jazzers in the biz—offered their written thoughts strictly out of the kindness of their hearts. I thank them for their beautiful words.

I'm honored and thrilled that so many former Jazz Messengers gave of their time. Joanne Brackeen, Donald Brown, Steve Davis, Essiet Okun Essiet, Robin Eubanks, Charles Fambrough, Benny Green, Donald Harrison, Freddie Hubbard, Geoffrey Keezer, Brian Lynch, Chuck Mangione, Wynton Marsalis, Mulgrew Miller, Billy Pierce, Lonnie Plaxico, Valery Ponomarev, David Schnitter, Horace Silver, Cedar Walton, and James Williams were uniformly insightful, interesting, generous, and, most importantly, as nice as could possibly be.

A whole heap of non-Messengers were also of great help:

Much appreciation to the fine folks at Black Saint/Soul Note Records in

Italy and Dragon Records in Sweden for their respective contributions to the Blakey Sideman CD Fund.

Jason Byrne at Third Floor Media and Kathey Marsella at Wilkins Management withstood many phone calls and emails with tolerance and grace.

Michael Fitzgerald and Steve Schwartz's *Chronology of Art Blakey and the Jazz Messengers* is an exhaustive work that saved me literally hundreds of hours of research. It's essential that all Messenger maniacs surf over to Michael's website (http://www.eclipse.net/~fitzgera/). It's the ultimate labor of love.

Michael Cuscuna, Sarah Lourie, and the wonderful staff at Mosaic Records let me spend one beautiful afternoon sifting through a bazillion breathtaking Francis Wolff pictures. Our of the goodness of his heart, Michael allowed me the use of over a dozen shots, including the lovely Blakey portrait on the cover. I appreciate that not just for me, but also for the readers who will have the opportunity to enjoy these beautiful pictures every time they open this book. *All Francis Wolff photographs—©Mosaic Images LLC—are available for purchase through www.mosaicgallery.com.*

Thanks to John Cerullo, Barbara Ritola, Dan Mausner, and all the fine folks at the Hal Leonard Corporation for their belief and enthusiasm. As any writer knows, the publishing business is a tough one, but the Leonard-ites have made the entire process as smooth as *Kind of Blue*.

Ben Schafer, my most excellent editor, is one of those guys who *gets it*. He's not a Messenger-phile, but he understands the impact that Art Blakey's collective had on not just the jazz world, but also the modern music world at large. Plus he likes the way I write, which demonstrates his excellent taste.

Finally, over half of this book was written at the home of my parents, Marvin and Maxine Goldsher, both of whom showed remarkable patience during an indescribably difficult time in my life. Words cannot do justice.

Author's Note

THROUGHOUT *Hard Bop Academy*, I will be citing dozens of songs to illustrate the concepts and styles of the Jazz Messengers here profiled. Rather than include a full discography at the back of the book, I've noted in the text which album each tune is culled from with complete information appearing at the song's first mention. This will eliminate the need to jump to the end of the book whenever you, the reader, are curious as to which session produced each song.

BRANFORD MARSALIS
Introduction to Hard Bop Academy

ART BLAKEY was not only one of the most important drummers in jazz, but one of the best bandleaders as well. It is not a coincidence that many of his sidemen went on to have successful careers in concert and on recordings.

The long list of Jazz Messengers is impressive indeed: Jackie McLean, Hank Mobley, Freddie Hubbard, Wayne Shorter, Lee Morgan, Benny Golson, Doug Watkins, Curtis Fuller, Valery Ponomarev, Bobby Watson, Wynton Marsalis, James Williams, Bill Pierce, Kenny Garrett, Donald Harrison, and Terence Blanchard are just a few of the scores of names associated with the Art Blakey legacy.

Mr. Goldsher's literary contribution to the jazz legacy is quite a unique one. While most books (naturally) focus on a bandleader or icon of an era, Mr. Goldsher chose to make the sidemen the stars. It should be a pleasure for you to learn about the man we called "Bu" from the people musically closest to him. Learn about his contributions to their development as musicians and their contributions to him, as well as their personal development as men on the road with Art.

For those of you who love the history of jazz from an insider's point of view, *Hard Bop Academy* is a must-read. These are memories and stories of the unsung heroes of American music: the sidemen.

BOBBY WATSON
Introduction to Hard Bop Academy

ART BLAKEY. Abdullah Ibn Buhaina. How can I put this into words? Do I have enough room?…

This introduction could have easily become a novel. I mean, I was up under Art's armpit for four and a half years, and I loved every minute of it. I knew that being a Jazz Messenger was a once-in-a-lifetime opportunity to learn. I tried my best to shadow Art's lifestyle, philosophy, and beliefs for the time I was with him. Some cats thought I was weak and kissed ass. I didn't see it that way—I saw myself as blessed. Art was faith in action. He walked with angels. "Don't worry, Bobby, the angels are with us," he would say. I would say, "Wow," and believe. I listened, I grew, and I developed my sound through the platform he provided for me on a nightly basis. How cool is that?

Whenever Art would enter a room, the ions in the air would change. He commanded respect, and gave *you* respect when you respected yourself. Many musicians were scared of him, scared to hang out with him because at some point, he would "read" you—by that I mean Art was an acute observer of human nature. He could size up a person faster than anyone I have ever met. This was amazing to me—at some point you could expect a brutally honest assessment of your musicianship and human strengths and weaknesses. It was the latter that frightened most of the musicians who worked with Art. Art loved me, that's for sure, and for that, I suffered some of his cruelest criticisms. Because to have Art's love was to get the truth, which wasn't always what you wanted to hear. And for that I am forever grateful.

I hung out 24/7 with him, listening to countless stories (some true, some not). I car-sat for him while he ran errands. I almost destroyed my marriage because of him, and I missed the birth of my firstborn child because I was in Spain on the road with him. Oh yes, there were great sacrifices. That was all part of being a Jazz Messenger.

He always used to say about his sidemen, "When these guys get too old, I'm going to get some new ones." When my time came to leave, we had our talk in a car headed back to New York. I had made twelve recordings and done countless tours around the planet with the man. He had more young lions to baptize before he hung up his sticks. "This isn't the post office, you know," he'd always say. I knew that my time with the great man was limited and I wanted to absorb as much of his vibe as I could, so I could try to remember and keep it alive. I mean, the direct connection to Charlie Parker, John Coltrane, Lee Morgan, Bud Powell, Thelonious Monk, the whole damn legacy, the story of jazz, was in this man. How could one not become intoxicated?

The lessons I learned from him will stick with me forever: I shun compliments now because of him. I do not look for praise after a solo because of him. I play my horn for myself first because of him. I can take it as well as dish it out because of him. He made a leader out of me, taught me how to use, observe, and elevate the musicians I hire. He taught me how to read the vibe of an audience, and how to use time. He taught me how to build a solo. He taught me the value of a *band*. And finally, the most important thing I learned: He taught me how to love myself.

You see, Art Blakey was a teacher, and his lessons must be preserved, which is why *Hard Bop Academy* is such a vital book. And Alan Goldsher is definitely the dude to write it, because he was there. He heard the band numerous times, and he was moved by what he saw—and that can't be explained to anybody who wasn't there. But I know Alan will do his best to try.

I am forever grateful. Long live Buhaina.

JAVON JACKSON
Introduction to Hard Bop Academy

FOR OVER forty years, Art Blakey and the Jazz Messengers were one of the predominant instrumental ensembles in the art form known as jazz. This musical group possessed and exemplified many tremendous qualities inherent to the rich tradition of America's only art form: the blues, sophisticated compositions, ensemble tightness, and cutting-edge improvisation.

One last attribute to mention—and in my opinion the most important—is that Art Blakey and the Jazz Messengers placed a heavy emphasis on the toe-tapping aspect of their music. Defined another way—THE GROOVE! It is with fond memories that I recall Art Blakey uttering this encouraging phrase to the band just prior to a performance: "Swing them to death." Art never took an opportunity to play his drums for granted, nor did he ever give his audience less than his maximum effort.

It was my sincere pleasure and privilege to have been a member of the Jazz Messengers featuring Art Blakey from 1987 until the legendary drummer's untimely death in 1990. My tenure with Art was filled with incredible experiences; upon sharing these experiences with other musicians who were once a part of this famed fraternity, stories and reflections would amazingly and amusingly mirror themselves. However, the difference always comes in the perspective, which I thoroughly enjoy.

Thus, it is with great enthusiasm that I welcome and support Alan Goldsher's endeavor of bringing the story of the Jazz Messengers to the public. Unquestionably, no Art Blakey, no Jazz Messengers, so the insights of these various artists focus on their vital connection and kinship with Mr. Blakey.

My first meeting with Alan, as well as all subsequent conversations, occurred over the telephone. Upon the initial call, Alan's huge respect and admiration for jazz—and specifically for the topic of Art Blakey and the Jazz Messengers—was very apparent. As our phone conversations grew in number, I continually found Alan to be absolute in his passion, vision, and resolve toward the completion of this daunting interview process.

I thank Alan for considering and requesting me to include my thoughts regarding Art Blakey and the Jazz Messengers, a period in my life that has shaped me in ways unimaginable; I was also happy and eager to write an introduction for this worthy project. There is no question that the words ahead reveal a tremendous range of emotions and viewpoints from the musicians who helped create the Harvard University of jazz, Art Blakey and the Jazz Messengers.

TERENCE BLANCHARD
Introduction to Hard Bop Academy

THE EXPERIENCE of being a sideman in Art Blakey's band was more like that of the student and the mentor. When people have asked me what it was like, I always tell them that in the four-year period that I was in the band, I felt that I had grown forty years.

Art taught me more about life and how to relate to people than anyone else in my life other than my father. He was the kind of secure person who could let you grow by letting you make the mistakes you had to make to understand. Two weeks of mishaps would teach you what could take two years of talking-to to learn. Art also had the talent of knowing exactly when it was best to talk to you. It was as if he could tell that you were at a cross-roads in your life and it was time for you to hear the truth about where you were as a musician and what you needed to do to obtain your goals.

Bu had this Zen-like quality of telling you the same stories over and over again to bring home various points that he felt were necessary to help you understand the lengths to which musicians have gone to develop their craft. These stories were repeated so much—it was like Chinese water torture—that one could mouth them word for word as they were being told. The interesting thing is that now that I have my own band, I find myself boring my sidemen with repeated tales told to me by Bu. Funny, though, they still work.

I will always be in his debt.

Love always…

Preface

I *FRIGGIN' LOVE* Art Blakey and the Jazz Messengers.

I was hipped to the band in 1981, back when I was still a wet-behind-the-ears jazz neophyte. *DownBeat* had just run a review of two recent Jazz Messengers records: *Straight Ahead* and *Album of the Year*. (If memory serves, the former received a five-star review, the latter, four-and-a-half.) The article made those two records out to be these miniature meteorites, hard bop bombs sent to Earth to destroy all that was wrong with the then-floundering acoustic jazz scene. The review went on to say that the Messengers sextet was a well-oiled machine and both albums should be counted as some of the finest old-school hard bop heard on wax in the past few years. Irresistible, right?

So I hit my parents up for an advance on my allowance, zipped over to the Jazz Record Mart—a big ol' jazz repository in downtown Chicago where I would ultimately be employed for six years—and scarfed up both albums.

They knocked me on my ass.

Powerful. Up-tempo. Melodic. Accessible. Blitzkrieg. Everything that a jazz fanatic in the making could ask for. Needless to say, I needed much more Messengerism. Luckily for me, the band at that point had been a jazz force for twenty-some-odd years, so there was much more Messengerism to be had.

My next Jazz Messengers purchase was the 1960 classic *A Night in Tunisia*. Great stuff. Wayne Shorter—whom at the time I thought of only as "That sax dude from Weather Report" (boy, was I jazz newbie)—entranced me, as did a certain funkdafied trumpet stud named Lee Morgan.

Just like that, I was addicted. Just like that, I had to have it all.

Over the next decade, I meticulously went about the business of tracking down every Art Blakey and the Jazz Messengers record that could be tracked down: new, used, bootlegs, airshots, vinyl, cassettes, CDs, anything and everything. And while Blakey's balls-to-the-wall timekeeping and phatter-than-phat press rolls were a huge part of the band's appeal, what always grabbed and held my attention was the ever-changing batch of sidemen. It got to the point where I mentally categorized my Messengers collection by their respective front lines: Benny Golson/Lee Morgan; Wayne Shorter/Freddie Hubbard/Curtis Fuller; Wynton Marsalis/Branford Marsalis/Billy Pierce.

But as I was a burgeoning bassist, it stood to reason that for me, the rhythm section—most specifically, the piano/bass combo—went a long way in defining and individualizing each session. Bobby Timmons and Jymie Merritt—*damn*! Cedar Walton and Reggie Workman—*hit me!* James Williams and Charles Fambrough—*bring it on!*

Dozens and dozens of stellar instrumentalists revolved in and out of the group, but no matter who was in the band, the Messengers always sounded like the Messengers. And this wasn't due strictly to Blakey's presence; it was because each group had a respect—nay, a *reverence*—for the cats that preceded them. You can trace a direct trumpet line from Kenny Dorham to Freddie Hubbard to Brian Lynch. Or a piano line from Horace Silver to Mulgrew Miller to Geoffrey Keezer. Or a bass line from Doug Watkins to Reggie Workman to Essiet Essiet.

And this draw-from-your-predecessor attitude wasn't specific to just the musicians' respective improvisations, it was also evident in the writing. The Messengers' compositional concept shaped and reshaped itself from year to year, from band to band, but even though the original tunes that each Messengers composer concocted were, well, original, they almost always were soaked with that harder-than-hard bop vibe. It can be said that Horace Silver's pen begat Benny Golson's pen begat Wayne Shorter's pen begat Bobby Watson's pen. And so on. And so on.

This lineage is the heart of *Hard Bop Academy*.

Hard Bop Academy is simply a fan's-eye view of one of jazz's most beloved, enduring ensembles. I tried to make the whole thing feel like Blakey's music: an organized jam session—funky, fiery, and, most importantly, fun.

What *Hard Bop Academy* is not is an Art Blakey biography—I'll leave that mammoth project to the true historians. And since more than 150 musicians graced the band—many of whom were never documented on record—this is not a rundown of each and every sideman. I had to pick and choose the artists who I felt had the biggest impact on the aforementioned lineage. It also should be said that *Hard Bop Academy* doesn't feature much in the way hardcore, in-depth musical analysis. While I cited a ton and a half of compositions to support specific points, I didn't dissect each song into bite-size pieces. My breakdowns are more in the spirit of, *This is why you should check out this tune*, rather than, *Shorter's juxtaposition of the C♯ minor melody and the F major bass part creates an Americana-rooted tension reminiscent of early-period Charles Ives*. This was a wholly subjective process, and—as is the case with all subjective processes—some will disagree with my choices. Which is cool, because disagreement sparks discussion, and discussion sparks passion. And if there's any jazz ensemble that merits passion, it's Art Blakey and the Jazz Messengers.

You'll dig this book if you think of me as the guy standing next to you in the jazz section of your local record store—the guy who picks up a copy of, say, *Free for All*, then gently elbows you in the side and says, "Hey, groove on this." When you ask why, I'd say, "Because Shorter is out of control!" Then I'd pause, and add, "If you're feeling this, you oughta check out *Moanin'*. Benny Golson tears it *up*."

From there, you'll be addicted. From there, you'll have to have it all.

CHAPTER 1

ART BLAKEY
The Messenger and His Message

"I'll play drums until Mother Nature tells me different. I'll retire when I'm six feet under."

—Art Blakey

AS IT TURNED OUT, Arthur Blakey spoke the truth. Blakey (a.k.a. Abdullah Ibn Buhaina, a.k.a. "Bu") was a musician from the very beginning until the absolute end.

Born in Pittsburgh, Pennsylvania, on October 11, 1919, Blakey taught himself how to play piano during his adolescence, then, as a precocious teenager, formed his own jazz big band. "I've had bands since I was fifteen years old," Blakey said. "I was playing piano with the best band in Pittsburgh—eighteen pieces—and the best gig, too. We sounded like Count Basie, Fletcher Henderson; we played Benny Goodman and Benny Carter things."

But young Art thought little of his burgeoning keyboard skills. "I used to play by ear. I used to play in five keys, and that was it. I didn't know *anything* about a piano." A fortuitous meeting with a local hoodlum knocked him off the piano bench and changed the course of jazz history. "I ended up being the drummer [in the band] because a gangster told me—with a .38—'You hit the drum.' And I said, 'This is my band. You don't tell me what to do. You're crazy.' He said, 'You want to work here, kid?' I said, 'Sure I want to work here.' He said, 'Then play the drums and don't argue with me.' So I went up there and played the drums. [Pittsburgh-born pianist] Erroll Garner came in and took my gig *and* my band."

1

By 1942, Art reckoned that he'd gone as far as he could go in his hometown, so with the help of a certain piano-giant-in-the-making, Blakey relocated to the jazz mecca of the world. "Thelonious Monk was responsible for me when I moved from Pittsburgh to New York City. He used to take me and [pianist] Bud Powell around to all the clubs to play. If the musicians didn't want us to sit in, [Monk] would run them off the stage, sit down, and play with me. At that time jobs were so few, and musicians had cliques. Times were tight, things were changing, but Monk was just outstanding in himself."

Blakey's percussive aptitude was undeniable, and he soon landed a gig with revered big band leader Fletcher Henderson. After a fruitful ten-month spell with Henderson, Art took a significant side trip to Beantown. "I lived in Boston during the war," Blakey said. "I had a big band up there." Fronting this band taught Art a number of business and life lessons that served him quite well. "There were a lot of musicians around there and they didn't know how to talk to people. Musicians are not good businessmen, and I know—I'm not a good businessman either, but I can bullshit. I know how to talk and get something done, to get things organized, get it going. So that's what happened and I stayed there. And then I joined 'B' from there, and we went on the road from there."

"B" was Billy Eckstine, and Blakey's three-year stint with the vocalist's groundbreaking bebop big band was a vital part of his musical development. Eckstine's troupe included such up-and-comers as trumpeters Dizzy Gillespie, Fats Navarro, and Miles Davis; saxophonists Charlie "Bird" Parker, Dexter Gordon, and Sonny Stitt; and vocalist Sarah Vaughan—no surprise, then, that the band was a hotbed of innovation. The leader offered his soloists room to stretch out and develop their pioneering ideas within the band's intricate arrangements, all of which gave Blakey the opportunity to concoct a drum style that combined large-group power with small-group musicality.

Two years after the Eckstine band disbanded—and after Blakey, thanks to a trip to Africa, converted to Islam and adopted the name Abdullah Ibn Buhaina—the drummer fronted the first group emblazoned with the Jazz Messengers imprint. "The Jazz Messengers really started in 1949, but then it was called the Seventeen Messengers," Blakey said. "The cats that put the band together came to me and told me I was going to be the leader. Being a musician has nothing to do with being a leader; I was a good organizer. That's always been my talent. The Seventeen Messengers was a good band; there were a lot of great players in it, like [tenor saxophonist] Sonny Rollins and Bud Powell. We were just playing around New York, making a few gigs, but economically the band was a disaster, so we had to break it up." Blakey spent the ensuing five years freelancing with such heavy hitters as Thelonious Monk, Charlie Parker, Miles Davis, Buddy DeFranco, and the Fats Navarro/Tadd Dameron band.

In 1954, the seeds were planted for what eventually became the archetypal Jazz Messengers format. "I went into Birdland with [trumpeter] Clifford Brown, [pianist] Horace Silver, [bassist] Curly Russell, and [alto saxophonist] Lou Donaldson for a few weeks," Blakey explained. We made some live, unrehearsed records and they did pretty well." Indeed, the Art Blakey Quintet's *A Night at Birdland, Volumes 1 & 2* (Blue Note, 1954) was an unqualified musical success, the first time that jazz fans had the chance to truly experience Blakey's authority as both a hard bop drummer and charismatic bandleader.

The canny Horace Silver saw the band's potential, and presented to Blakey the possibility of taking his hard bop concept one step further. "It was Horace who decided we should organize a group," Blakey said. "He got [tenor saxophonist] Hank Mobley and [trumpeter] Kenny Dorham and [bassist] Doug Watkins and myself and said, 'Art, you should be the leader since you have more experience than the rest of the guys and we'd like to have you up here with us.' And I said, 'Well, what should we call the band?' He said, 'We can't call it Seventeen Messengers, so we'll call it Art Blakey and the Jazz Messengers.' And that's the way the band started and this is what Horace named it, and it's stuck ever since."

The first batch of Messengers remained intact until 1956, when Silver left to form his quintet. "It first started out being a cooperative thing," Blakey noted, "but it didn't work because it wasn't equal. I had the weight and it had to go my way and Horace went out on his own and that's when we began to bring different cats in. I just kept goin' with it. I thought, *Well, somebody got to stay here and keep the shop*."

And a fine shopkeeper he was.

Part of Blakey's triumph as a bandleader stems from his Zen-ish approach to bandleading. "I don't tell [my sidemen] what to play—I tell them what *not* to play: Don't try to play everything you know in one chorus; don't try to make a career out of one tune. When you're playing and you get to a climax, you stop. You can't build to another climax after you've made one. So you stop, and maybe next tune you'll get another climax—or maybe not. It's only once or twice a month you really get to play, you really feel in your heart what you play—it isn't something you hit every night. So you just play, and try not to drop below a certain level, and maybe once or twice a month you'll go over that—you're feeling good, the audience is throwing them vibes back, there ain't nothing for you to do but blow your brains out. It's beautiful."

Blakey was initially stunned by the Messengers' success. "We didn't expect the band to go worldwide and make a lot of money—we were just trying to make some gigs and play, because we were tired of goin' on gigs and jamming with a pickup band, playing the same old tunes. People got tired of that shit and I could see they were getting tired, and I don't like chaos anyhow. I like freedom, but without discipline, it's chaos. So we wrote arrangements, got sharp, got some suits, started paying attention to the audience, and put it together."

Though it was a drummer who fronted the Jazz Messengers, the Jazz Messengers were never a drum-oriented group. "I don't like long solos—long drum solos I especially don't like," Blakey said. "As a drummer, you can't be in competition with a soloist. If a soloist is thinking of something, trying to connect something together, and you make a lot of noise, he'll forget it. Now he's gotta think of something else in a split second; that makes it very hard."

Blakey was (and is) acknowledged as a talent scout second to none—he gave first opportunities to such diversely styled future stars as trumpeter Wynton Marsalis, tenor saxophonist Benny Golson, and pianist Keith Jarrett, among *many* others—but much of the Messengers' revolving-door approach came from a purely practical place. "When a guy got big, I'd have to fire him, because I couldn't afford to pay him," Blakey complained. "Then I'd just grab anybody. But I'd pick 'em out, I'd find out where they come from, because I don't put musicians together just because they're good musicians. It has to be a spiritual thing—they have to like each other. I don't want a musician in the band who thinks he's greater than everybody else; if he does, he has no business being there." (In that spirit, Art was possibly proudest of the 1958 edition of the Messengers. "I like the Lee Morgan/Bobby Timmons/Benny

Golson group. They were fantastic musicians, they were gentlemen, they acted like gentlemen, they didn't believe in being late for a performance, they didn't believe in getting on the stage with their anger.")

The combination of discipline, tight arrangements, well-organized set lists, brilliant soloists, fat-free solos, and, above all, an uncanny ability to wail their hindquarters off on a nightly basis made Art Blakey's Jazz Messengers one of the most popular—if not the single most popular— straight-ahead jazz combos of the modern era. (Then again, it's possible that said popularity stems solely from Blakey's badass-edness. "I keep my foot in [my musicians'] behinds every night. I scare 'em to death.")

As for Blakey's prediction that he'd play until he was six feet under? He was off by only five months—he played his final gigs as leader of the Jazz Messengers in July of 1990, and he died later that year, on October 16. Upon hearing of Blakey's death, ex-Messengers alto saxophonist Jackie McLean said, "The school is closed for good."

Jackie indeed knew of what he spoke; but Headmaster Blakey's lessons and legacy will live on through the sidemen who graduated from the Hard Bop Academy.

CHAPTER 2

THE TRUMPETERS
High Modes

"I admired every trumpeter in the Jazz Messengers. All of us trumpeters had the Art Blakey sound, but at the same time, we were being groomed for individuality."

—Chuck Mangione

EVEN AN acknowledged saxophone stud like Branford Marsalis was thoroughly envious of the attention garnered by the trumpeters who played with Art Blakey and the Jazz Messengers. "Virtually every one of his meal tickets during the history of the band was a trumpet player—Lee Morgan, Freddie Hubbard, et cetera. When Wayne Shorter was in the band, he was an ancillary figure, even though he wrote most of the music."

Valery Ponomarev—himself a not-too-shabby meal ticket—agreed with Branford's assessment. "Art Blakey loved all instruments, but he had a special affinity for the trumpet."

Why? Maybe it was a logistical thing—volume-wise, the trumpet was the only traditional acoustic jazz instrument that could consistently compete with Blakey's authoritarian drums. Freddie Hubbard, one of the most potent brassmen to ever grace the group, noted that Buhaina's percussive tirades rattled even a chopmeister such as himself. "Art Blakey was so domineering and so strong as both a player and a person that at first I was kind of frightened. He wanted all the trumpet players to play with bravado, to be out front and lead. I'd heard him play behind Clifford Brown and Kenny Dorham and Bill Hardman. All those guys, they had to play *so hard*; it took me about two years to get my chops in shape for Art. At first, I'd blow myself out in the first set—

I used to go home and soak my chops in some ice. After a while, I got used to it." Ultimately, according to Hubbard, the nightly arse-kicking paid off. "Art Blakey has helped more trumpet players develop their own individual styles than *anybody*."

As the final Messengers trumpeter, Brian Lynch was possibly best suited to take a big-picture view of the trumpet chair. "The idea of the Messengers was a progressive one, in terms of style; the style was never something that became fixed. That's why the trumpet players in the '80s, like Wynton Marsalis and Terence Blanchard and Wallace Roney, made such good statements with the band. Even though every Jazz Messengers trumpeter was Messenger-like, you could always hear the new trumpet styles coming through the band.

"I wish it was still going on."

OSMOSIS
Kenny Dorham

"Kenny Dorham was the predecessor to all the trumpet players who became true Jazz Messengers."

—Valery Ponomarev

HOW DO you describe Kenny Dorham's trumpet sound?

Crystalline? That's an apt word, no doubt, but Kenny's skittering tone is more crystalline than crystal. If that's possible.

Sweet-tart? Not bad, but Dorham's palate is wide enough to include salt, spice, and—you guessed it—everything nice.

Genial? You betcha, but that's too small a word to illustrate the scope of K.D.'s positivity.

Dorham's sound is so alluring, so individualistic, so *right*, that we'll just have to go with an "all of the above."

Which brings up the question, How does a crystalline, sweet-tart, genial, alluring, individualistic, all-of-the-above trumpeter make his relatively subtle style work alongside Hurricane Art?

It boiled down to a combination of conviction and coolness. Before hooking up with the Messengers in 1954, Dorham had previously shared the bandstand with bebop deity Charlie Parker, and if you can hold your own with Charlie Parker—which Kenny did quite nicely—you can hold your own with Art Blakey. Which Dorham did for his entire one-year spell as a Messenger.

Still, it took a bit of restraint from Buhaina to give K.D.'s voice the breathing room necessary for him to flourish in the then-still-developing Messengers' scheme, a selfless act by Blakey that Terence Blanchard found quite admirable. "Kenny Dorham had a very lyrical sound, a very melodic kind of quality, which was always very interesting in that band, considering the power that that band played with. It really spoke to Art's musicianship, and to how flexible he was." Indeed, during Kenny's brief but effective spot on the Dorham original "Minor's Holiday" (*The Jazz Messengers at the Café Bohemia, Volumes 1 & 2*, Blue Note, 1955) Buhaina minimalistically complements the trumpeter's skittering lines with just his ride cymbal, his snare, and his hi-hat, before adding in a few well-timed tom-tom fills at the apex of Kenny's final chorus.

Chuck Mangione, himself a master of delicacy, concurred with Blanchard's assessment of Blakey's ability to prod his trumpeters into playing to his strengths. "If you could sit on top of what Art was playing—the wonderful groove that he laid down—you could play one note for a whole chorus and have a good time with it. Which was perfect for Dorham, because he wasn't a person who was screaming on the horn, he was a person who could make music within a limited range." This is exemplified on Kenny's *Café Bohemia* ballad feature "Yesterdays" (a tune that Dorham had a special affinity for, introducing it as a "very, very beautiful Jerome Kern original." Note the two "verys"). Kenny plays the stately, whole-note-filled melody without adornment; his improv is also a portrait of elegance—even his forays to the top of his middle register have that distinctly Dorham-ish simmering mellowness. All in all, a textbook example of what Mangione aptly described as "sitting on top of what Art was playing."

Chuck was also impressed with Kenny's inimitability, his inherent Dorham-ness. "As soon as K.D. played one note, you knew it was him. He had this very airy, wonderful sound; he was a very melodic player." That buoyancy is in full effect on Horace Silver's gospel-tinged "Doodlin'" (*Horace Silver and the Jazz Messengers*, Blue Note, 1954). Running blues scales left and right, Dorham goes to church with a minimum of notes and a maximum of, well, airiness. (Dorham's spacious sound is bolstered in part by the natural echo provided by Blue Note house engineer Rudy Van Gelder.)

In what would become S.O.P. for the Jazz Messengers, Dorham imparted his wisdom upon his followers; in this case, eventual Blakey-ite Freddie Hubbard was the beneficiary of his forerunner's savoir-faire. "Kenny told me, '[When you're playing with Blakey], lay back a little bit on volume, otherwise you'll blow yourself out.'" Freddie also was stirred by Dorham's relentless inventiveness. "He had a beautiful way of playing through chord changes, and he would play phrases that would go ten bars at a time." (In the earliest days of hard bop, most musicians played their phrases in multiples of four bars.) "Kenny also taught me how to get through an 'I Got Rhythm' bridge." A trip back to the Bohemia reveals that K.D. was a great guy to coach that particular set of chord changes; Hank Mobley's "Deciphering the Message" features a slightly modified "I Got Rhythm" middle eight, which Dorham dances over with aplomb during each of his four solo choruses.

Dorham received heaps of critical acclaim throughout his career (and not just because he was a jazz critic himself), but like many heady artists in any medium, his greatest popularity came after his death. "For me, Kenny Dorham was one of the most influential trumpet players in my development," Brian Lynch said, "even though he was someone I came to a little bit later. The original trumpet players coming out of the Art Blakey tradition that I first listened to were Lee Morgan, Freddie Hubbard, and Woody Shaw. But at a certain point in my development—around the same time that I really started becoming aware of Sonny Rollins's playing—I got to Kenny Dorham. He had real creativity and finesse in running the [chord] changes."

Wynton Marsalis succinctly summed up what K.D. was all about: "Kenny Dorham had a real interesting way of playing harmonies. He had a lot of soul."

Soul. And a crystalline/sweet-tart/genial tone. And an unshakable sense of individualism.

In other words, Kenny Dorham had "all of the above."

HIGH AND FLIGHTY
Donald Byrd

"Donald Byrd played like he believed."

—Wynton Marsalis

DONALD BYRD is *looooved.*

Just ask Terence Blanchard: "Donald Byrd added a great deal to that band. And his relationship with Blakey was a special one, all the way up until Art died. Byrd and Art were very close."

Just ask Valery Ponomarev: "Donald Byrd was a great Messenger, no question. He played beautiful phrases and beautiful jazz music, and they were already in the Jazz Messengers style, even at that point."

Just ask Wynton Marsalis: "Donald Byrd is very intelligent; he has a beautiful way of playing. He could play the blues, and he has a real leader-type of personality."

And just ask Freddie Hubbard: "Donald Byrd is my big brother. He was a business type of cat. Byrd was a big part of perpetuating that group. I love Donald Byrd."

All this *loooove* is both understandable and justifiable, because, as supported by his work with the Jazz Messengers, Donald Byrd is eminently lovable.

Byrd's stay with the Messengers was brief—approximately seven months, beginning in late 1955—and he waxed only one record with the band (*The Jazz Messengers*, Columbia, 1956), but his impact on the group was, if not profound, then at the very least sizable.

Without fail, each of his solos on the 1956 session run the hard bop gamut: the up-tempo pieces are furious displays of chops, swing, and fire, while the slow and medium-tempo numbers are models of restraint. He's *way* all over the horn on Hank Mobley's *way* up-tempo "Infra-Rae." He's melodically wild (or wildly melodic) on Silver's "Nica's Dream." On the Styne/Cahn standard "It's You or No One," he's vibrant and edgy. On Silver's "Ecaroh," he bulls over the unconventional changes with palpable conviction. On Mobley's "Carol's Interlude," he faultlessly eases his way through an atypical twenty-four-bar form. And on the radically reworked rendition of "The End of a Love Affair," he busts out a handful of Dizzy Gillespie licks. On the whole, a striking show of hard bop correctness.

Brian Lynch pointed out several reasons why Byrd was a hand-in-glove fit for Bu's boys. "His attention to detail and to ensemble playing was really important to the Jazz Messengers. He's an important figure in terms of his excellence and his consistency." According to Lynch, Byrd's impact on his instrument only grew as his career progressed. "Donald was somebody who kept up with the developments in the language; his playing and writing always was undergoing changes. He utilized more modern and angular melodic formations. Donald Byrd had a great effect on a lot of trumpet players. During the late '50s, he was about the most recorded trumpeter on the scene. Because of that, he was a great influence on the players that were coming up, especially Freddie Hubbard. Donald was a great all-around jazz trumpet player, a great hard bop trumpet player."

A great hard bop trumpet player who is *looooved*.

FOCUS
Bill Hardman

"Bill Hardman, bless his soul."

—Freddie Hubbard

IN 1949, a twenty-seven-year-old Cuban expatriate third baseman named Saturnino Orestes Arrieta Armas ("Minnie") Minoso made the jump from the Negro League's New York Cubans to the Major League's Cleveland Indians. In 1951, Minoso was dealt to the Chicago White Sox, with whom he spent the subsequent seven seasons. The remainder of the decade found him back in Cleveland; then, in 1960, he was returned to the White Sox. He wore a St. Louis Cardinals uniform in 1962, a Washington Senators outfit in 1963, and a White Sox jersey in 1964.

In 1976, Minnie suited up with the Sox for three games. In 1980, Minnie suited up with the Sox for two games.

To sum up: Minnie Minoso played professional baseball in the 1940s, the 1950s, the 1960s, the 1970s, and the 1980s.

Bill Hardman was the Minnie Minoso of the Jazz Messengers.

The respected, respectful trumpeter played with Blakey's band in the 1950s, the 1960s, the 1970s, and the 1980s. He didn't match Minoso's five decades in the limelight, but if Bill and Bu had lived deeper into the 1990s, there's no doubt they would have shared a stage and/or a studio at some point during that ten-year span.

Bill sidled onto the jazz scene in the early 1950s straight out of high school; his first high-profile gigs were with Jackie McLean and Charles Mingus. Unfortunately for Hardman—a hard-luck chap who was the victim of bad timing throughout his long and dignified career—he arrived onto the scene when both Miles Davis and Chet Baker were at the top of their powers, so, like many trumpeters of that era, Hardman carried out his business under some considerable shadows. But when he joined the Messengers for the first time in 1957, those in the know took notice. "Bill began to develop what ultimately became the Messengers trumpet style," Terence Blanchard said, "that powerful, strong trumpet playing that was needed to be in that band."

That power and strength was a boon for the fledgling group, and Blakey soon developed a special affinity for Hardman (Wynton Marsalis noted, "Art loved Bill Hardman, both as a player and a person"). This love and respect are understandable, considering Hardman's early stylistic resemblance to the horn-man who filled the trumpet seat in Bu's very first quintet. "He was about the closest to Clifford Brown in terms of his ideas on the trumpet," Freddie Hubbard said. Brian Lynch agreed, stating, "Bill was very expressive, coming out of the Clifford Brown school. He also had a certain sort of wit in his playing." (Valery Ponomarev is the lone dissenting voice regarding the Brownie/Hardman analogy. "Bill Hardman wasn't Clifford Brown—but he was still a *great* player.")

Bill's Brown-isms are apparent on his searing original composition "Theory of Art" (*A Night in Tunisia/Play Lerner and Lowe*, BMG Collectables, 2001). Throughout this 1957 session—and on that tune in particular—Hardman echoes, if not flat-out rips off, a number of Clifford licks; what raises Hardman above the level of mimicry is his distinctive manner of laying out his notes. "His phrasing gave him a little bit more of an elliptical sound," Lynch said, a quality that's also clear on both "The Biddie Griddies" and "Pot Pourri" (*Reflections of Buhaina*, Savoy, 1957). While a large percentage of Bill's lines are indeed straight out of Clifford's bag o' tricks, his agreeably choppy delivery gave him a style he could call his own.

Even at that early point in the Messengers' history, Hardman had a sense of the impending lineage; in that spirit, Bill—like Kenny Dorham—took Freddie Hubbard under his wing. "When I was trying to learn some of the Messenger songs," Hubbard said, "I would go over to his house and practice with him." (While hanging out at the House of Hardman, Freddie noticed something odd about the way his mentor physically approached his instrument. "It always amazed me how he could play from the side of his mouth, and play that well.") As it so happened, Freddie inadvertently reciprocated Bill's tutoring; for Hardman's second trip through Messengerland, which kicked off in 1967, listeners had to have been stunned by his out-of-left-field Hubbard-esque progressiveness. On "Slide's Delight," (*Moanin'*, Laserlight, 1968) Hardman is downright modernistic, personalizing a number of Hubbard's trademark rhythmic devices, most notably lengthy trills and/or eighth-note runs capped off with a clarion whole-note blast. That said, Hardman still had a toe in the hard bop ocean, and his periodic Brownian runs stand in sharp contrast to the unabashed modernisms delivered by his front-line mates, tenor saxophonist Billy Harper and trombonist Julian Priester.

Bill left the band again in 1968, only to return in 1970; he was then in and out—mostly in—with the Messengers for the next five years. Blanchard theorized that his lack of widespread notoriety during his third ride with the band stemmed from Hardman's career-long bugaboo—being in the wrong musical place at the wrong musical time. "He didn't get the credit he deserved in the 1970s. I think a lot of that had to do with the actual timing of when he joined the band; when he got in the band the third time, it was when fusion was on the way in, so nobody was really focusing on straight-ahead jazz."

Hindsight being 20/20, Hardman is more recognized for his contributions to the band by the second-generation Messengers trumpeters. And while Hubbard or Lee Morgan are cited as primary muses, Hardman was a solid secondary influence, if not for his playing, then for his work ethic. "Bill Hardman was a workhorse," Terence Blanchard said.

All in all, when you booted up Hardman: Version 1.9.5.7., you'd have yourself a few megs of Kenny Dorham, a few megs of Donald Byrd, and a few megs of Clifford Brown; for Hardman: Version 1.9.6.8., he downloaded some Freddie Hubbard into his hard-driving hard drive. And while his musicality was unquestioned, it was his longevity that was his hallmark. When it comes to the Jazz Messengers, "Bill Hardman" is synonymous with "comeback." And who knows—the cat might just be resilient enough to come back again.

SEARCH FOR THE NEW LAND
Lee Morgan

"Lee Morgan would sit up there and wiggle his valves on one note, and Art would be bashing away like a crazy person. That shit must have been off the hook when you heard it for the first time."
—Terence Blanchard

IF KENNY DORHAM, Donald Byrd, and Bill Hardman set the table for impending Messengers trumpeters, than Lee Morgan cooked the meal.

And he cooked it but good.

"The trumpet player who *really* created the sound of the Jazz Messengers was Lee Morgan," Valery Ponomarev said. "His phrasing, his tongue attack—amazing."

"Lee had a lot to do with what came to be known as the Blakey style," Terence Blanchard said. "His was the first incarnation of the band that really made a lot of noise. Lee gave the band a certain kind of passion and fire that you hadn't seen much of prior to him but you sure saw a lot of after he left."

A no-holds-barred prodigy, the Philly-born Morgan had barely turned eighteen when he hooked up with one of the most exalted trumpeters of the modern era. "I first heard Lee when he was playing with Dizzy Gillespie's big band," Chuck Mangione said. "Lee had a brilliant, happy-sounding, funky approach to the trumpet. He was a phenomenon right off the bat." During his two-year stay with Gillespie, Morgan absorbed enough modern jazz history to get a jump on his career; before he enlisted with the Messengers, he'd already laid down a series of records for Blue Note that exhibited his almost-in-full-bloom style.

His early aptitude is one of the reasons that Bill Hardman believed Morgan would be a model Jazz Messenger. In another example of the whole Blakey lineage thing, the pre-Morgan Messengers trumpeter handpicked his own replacement. "Bill Hardman was the one who went and got Lee Morgan and brought him to the band," Blakey said. "Bill said, 'I think he's better for the band than I am. He's young and he's gonna be great.'" (It's also been said that tenor saxophonist Benny Golson invited Morgan to join the group at the same time he brought in fellow Philadelphians pianist Bobby Timmons and bassist Jymie Merritt. *Hmmm…*)

Lee was in and out of the band between 1957 and 1964, and though he shared the front line with a number of saxophonists, and though his primary partner in crime was Wayne Shorter, he not only coexisted but thrived next to both Golson and Hank Mobley, in spite of their divergent saxophonic concepts.

While each edition featuring Morgan delivered a flock of original compositions—some of which would become cornerstones of the Messengers book—Lee's musical flexibility is best gleaned on the standard tunes. The trumpeter stood beside Mobley during the 1959 burner ...*At the Jazz Corner of the World*; on the Monk-penned "Justice" (which is based on the chord changes of "Just You, Just Me"), he tweaks his tone so it sounds uncannily like Mobley's eventual employer, Miles Davis. On "Come Rain or Come Shine" (*Moanin'*, Blue Note, 1958), his Gillespie-esque drawn-out intervallic runs are the perfect complement to Golson's Coleman Hawkins-ish glissandos.

(As it happened, *Moanin'* was the album that truly put Lee Morgan on the jazz map. "When that record came out, Lee was more popular than Miles," Freddie Hubbard claimed. And while Freddie's assessment may be colored by his palpable love for his forerunner in the band, Morgan's star did indeed rise upon its release. And not only did the album increase his visibility, but the title cut had consequences for each and every future Messengers trumpeter: After the band glided through the call-and-response melody, Lee kicked off his solo with one of the baddest one-bar gospel-bop licks in the history of one-bar gospel-bop licks: *Beep bwop boo-da*. The end of his solo concludes with an inverted reprise of the phrase: *Da boo bwop-beep*. Eventually, "Moanin'" became one of Blakey's signature songs—he performed it almost every night up until the end—and Morgan's intro and outro bars were so memorable and crowd-pleasing that every Messengers trumpeter thereafter began and ended his "Moanin'" solo with his version of those licks.)

Though he melded easily with Benny and Hank, Lee Morgan didn't truly become *Lee Morgan* until Wayne Shorter joined the band. Their mutual respect was evident both in the way they harmonized during ensemble passages and they way they instrumentally prodded one another. Tenor saxophonist Clifford Jordan's composition "Lost and Found" (*The Witch Doctor*, Blue Note, 1961) is a snapshot of Morgan and Shorter's musical camaraderie: They managed the knotty fourteen-bar blues head with the greatest of ease;

then, after Shorter's typically heady improv, Morgan slithers and boils for a couple of choruses before launching into a blinding string of eighth-note runs that crash beautifully against Wayne's space-filled lines.

Predictably, Shorter adored Morgan's melding of the recent past and impending future. "Lee was different. A lot of his licks came from Clifford [Brown], or Fats [Navarro], or Dizzy, and so many others. But he was original, so adaptable. He had the sound to overcome anything, and he knew how to get hot quick. He knew how to 'write a letter.'"

Wynton Marsalis also recognized and revered Morgan's stylistic mélange. "Lee Morgan played a lot like Clifford Brown—he played a hard-driving, crackling trumpet, a singing trumpet, a brash trumpet, a real kind of cocky trumpet. But he also took more of the elements of blues—he used bluesy type of effects, like bending notes and stuff like that. He had a really big sound, and he played great within the time."

Freddie Hubbard agreed with Wynton's assessment. "Lee Morgan was one of the greatest trumpet players. He was one of *the* best, if not the best, trumpet players to play with Art. When I heard him when I first came to New York, I got ready to go back to Indianapolis. He had a little Clifford, he had a little of everything, but he had his own little style. I have the utmost respect for him. He was really incredible. I don't think I reached that level—but I took it into another direction." (Brian Lynch noted that Hubbard made no secret of his humbleness in the face of Morgan's onslaught: "Freddie once told me, 'People say I have a big sound, but I think Lee had a *much* bigger sound than I did.'") Hubbard had three simple reasons why he felt Morgan was so damn good: "He was tricky. He had a great embouchure. And he was a cocky little guy."

Antithetically, this "cocky little guy" was modest about his own skills. "I don't think I have a completely original style, though I do have an identity," Morgan said. "An identity is when someone who knows jazz can say, 'That's Lee Morgan playing.' But my basic style is comprised of a strong Fats Navarro/Clifford Brown influence, and Miles and Dizzy, and then again a Bud [Powell] and a Bird thing. I think a definite style comes with living and experience and traveling until you play what you are, you play yourself on the horn."

Wynton and Freddie were both aware of Morgan's cockiness simply because the manner in which Morgan attacks his horn is *way* cocky, a factor that's in evidence on the Messengers' multiple recordings of "It's Only a Paper Moon." On the standard, which ultimately became one of Lee's show-pieces, he abuses the changes both in the studio (*The Big Beat*, Blue Note, 1960) and in concert (*Lausanne 1960: 2nd Set*, TCB Records, 1996). In each case, he sets up his swaggering take on the melody with a declaratory trill; after Shorter's think-piece solo spots, Morgan's brassy, blues-rooted outbursts are a breath of funky-fresh air. But on the extended live version, he radiates that cockiness, assertive both during his first-chorus murmur and his second- and third-chorus shrieks.

Another Blakey standard that bore Morgan's fingerprints (or lip prints) was Gillespie's "A Night in Tunisia." "I heard Lee and Wayne playing 'Tunisia' one night when I went to Birdland, and it scared me to death," Hubbard said. "Art Blakey was playing so hard that he drove everybody off the stage—except Lee, who stayed right there with him." Of the many versions of "Tunisia" cut by Messengers bands featuring Morgan, the standout version can be found on an album called—are you ready for this?—*A Night in Tunisia* (Blue Note, 1960). It's played at a tempo far faster than Dizzy intended, and the "A" section—a vamp-ish set of chord changes that allows for maximum wailing—gave Lee the opportunity to showcase the breadth of his talent, be it his mammoth tone, his devastating chops, or his rhythmic rightness. "I've always played a lot of notes, and now I'm getting space and those long lines," Morgan explained. "You want a change of sound, like trying to play little songs on a song, and that kind of thing. I want to play all over the horn and have a big, beautiful sound."

Compositionally, Morgan didn't put pen to manuscript paper nearly as often as Shorter, which is no shame; if you look up the word *prolific* in the dictionary, one of its definitions is "Wayne Shorter, circa early 1960s." But when Lee did write, he'd almost always nail it. He was eminently comfortable with waltzes, thus his finest Messengers tunes are in 3/4 time: "Kozo's Waltz" (*A Night in Tunisia*, Blue Note, 1960) is a speedy altered blues highlighted by some clever unison harmonies; "Blue Lace" (*The Freedom Rider*, Blue Note, 1961) is an evocative medium-tempo chordal maze, at once complex and hooky; and the Afro-bluesy "Calling Miss Khadija" (*Indestructible!*, Blue Note, 1964) is possibly the grooviest waltz in the history of waltzes. (Freddie Hubbard noted that Morgan's best tunes were deceptively demanding. "He could write hits. Some of those songs he wrote, they were funky, but the articulation was difficult.")

Wayne Shorter had an up-close-and-personal view of Morgan's compositional process. "His approach to writing was fundamental. He was much more at home playing than writing, but he would never ask for help [when he wrote]. That's one thing I dug about Lee—he would struggle through on his own. He knew that if he was too tutored as a writer, that he would sound contrived. So he kept his shortcomings and learned to communicate [via his writing] in spite of them."

Of course in the end, it was Morgan's blowing that resonated with the Messengers of the future. "Lee is a very important part of the Messenger trumpet tradition," Lynch said, "with his emotion that he put into his playing, and his communicativeness. When he was in the band, people used to think he was Art Blakey, because he just *had* to be the leader. He had charisma and style dripping from every pore." Little wonder that listeners believed Morgan to be the frontman, because, as Blakey himself noted, "Lee Morgan was always out front directing the music."

Nobody will dispute that Lee radiated charisma; the real question is, how did Morgan fit in so perfectly during each and every Messengers session he hit? Most likely because his musical soul merged an open mind with a sense of cool. "I don't like labels," Lee said. "If you can play, you can play with everybody. Whatever you prefer, you'll find sufficient quantities of talented musicians who prefer the same. But you should never limit your mind. There are no natural barriers. It's all music. It's either hip or it ain't."

Lee Morgan was hip. 'Nuff said.

But hipness wasn't Morgan's sole legacy. "He also affected the future sound of the band if only because of his effect on Freddie Hubbard," Marsalis said. In that vein, if Dorham, Byrd, and Hardman set the table for Lee Morgan, then Morgan set the table not just for Hubbard, but for *everybody*. "After Lee, the Jazz Messenger trumpet chair was filled by a whole constellation of geniuses," Ponomarev said. "One after another, after another, after another."

THE INTREPID FOX
Freddie Hubbard

"Freddie Hubbard was brash, Freddie Hubbard had bravura, and Freddie Hubbard was swinging."

—Wynton Marsalis

HERE'S ANOTHER baseball analogy:

Freddie Hubbard was to Lee Morgan what Mickey Mantle was to Joe DiMaggio. (It's also fair to say that Buhaina's Messengers were to jazz what the New York Yankees were/are to baseball.)

When the Commerce Comet replaced the Yankee Clipper in center field, the Bronx Bombers didn't lose a step. In fact, they leapt into a new era (not necessarily a better era—the previous era had been pretty damn good—but an era that was undeniably more modern). Most importantly, they kept winning.

Same deal with the Morgan/Hubbard baton pass. Hubbard drew from Morgan just the way that Mantle drew from DiMaggio. Noting this continuum, Wynton Marsalis said, "Freddie continued the trumpet tradition set by Lee. He brought that big sound, he had great phrasing, and he had a sense of being extremely modern."

For the young Hubbard, becoming a Messenger was the prototypical dream come true. "I used to listen to Art Blakey when I was back in [my hometown of] Indianapolis. When he had that group with Donald Byrd, Hank Mobley, Horace Silver, and Doug Watkins, I had a group with [saxophonist] James Spaulding and [bassist] Larry Ridley, and we took all those [Jazz Messengers] songs off the records. That was our gig music—we played those tunes at all our jobs."

Having a number of Messengers tunes under his belt helped prepare Hubbard for the inevitable. "When I moved to New York, I went down to Birdland to hear Art Blakey. Lee Morgan was in the band. They were playing so great. Fortunately, Lee had just recorded that record *The Sidewinder*, and he was about to leave the band. I was hanging around all the time, and I was able to learn the book. One night I was in a club, checking them out, and Art came up to me and said, 'Lee's leaving to start his own band, here's all the music.' I went back to Brooklyn, and I didn't stop smiling for a week. I was going to be playing with one of my idols! I had a chance to practice with

Doug Watkins—he lived near me in Brooklyn—and he helped me with some of the music. I was so excited that all the older cats came to my aid, trying to get me to cool out."

When he joined the band in 1961, Hubbard was a mere stripling of twenty-one, but his proficiency was so stunning that the jazz world couldn't help but notice. "When Freddie hit the scene, there was nobody out there doing what he was doing," Terence Blanchard said. "What was interesting about Freddie coming into the band after Lee Morgan was that Lee was *real* popular. But when Freddie joined, he came in there with his own power. He would do some of Lee's stuff, but he'd also be playing his long lines. It brought a different type of power to the band."

"Freddie Hubbard took it to the next level," Valery Ponomarev said. "His rhythmic approach was so accurate, so precise. His precision was incredible—ridiculous, really. Like Jack Nicholson said to Susan Sarandon in the film *The Witches of Eastwick*, 'Without precision, there's chaos.' Precision is the foundation of passion."

This precision is made apparent throughout even Hubbard's earliest Messengers sessions. Freddie's lone chorus on the up-tempo, style-shifting title cut of *Mosaic* (Blue Note, 1961) is a picture of exactitude, showcasing his pinpoint articulation and his rhythmic meticulousness, and his five choruses on the medium-tempo, style-shifting title cut of *Three Blind Mice* (Blue Note, 1962) are crisp and confident, and—in a subconscious shout-out to Lee Morgan—cocky.

Rapid BPM's were Hubbard's meat and potatoes, but, as Wynton Marsalis pointed out, "Freddie could play beautiful on a ballad. Like 'Skylark.'" Indeed, Hubbard's statement of the melody on the Hoagy Carmichael/Johnny Mercer classic (*Caravan*, Original Jazz Classics, 1962) is a portrait of self-possession; though his high-register double-time fills are hyper, they never compromise the tune's purity.

Hubbard came into the Messengers already performing at a high level, but he believes Blakey's brawn helped catapult him to an even higher plane. "I had played with Philly Joe Jones, and Philly Joe was just about the hippest small-group drummer [at the time]. But the fills that Art Blakey played with our unit, he made us sound like a big band. I used to stand off to the side and watch him play, and I'd say to myself, 'Look at this cat.' When he would do one of those press rolls, it would send chills from the floor, through my feet, then up to my brain. When he first did that [after I joined the band], he scared me to death. I was out there soloing, and he hit that press roll, and I went, *'Aaaaauuugh!* Goddamn, what's going on?' He's the only drummer in the world that I've heard or played with who could get the tension, build it, and keep the momentum moving forward without rushing the tempo. People misconstrue Art Blakey's volume—yeah, he would get loud sometimes, but it was a listenable loud. He would bash sometimes and get carried away, but he knew how to do fills and make it feel good."

Another pearl of wisdom Buhaina imparted upon Hubbard was that of brevity—and this particular nugget of knowledge was passed on the hard way. "[During live shows], I'd be taking about thirty choruses, and Art would say, 'Freddie, why d'you play so long? That ain't hip.' One time, I got off the stage and he said, 'This ain't your band. Wayne's the star.' So I said, 'Fine. I quit.' Then he hit me upside my head—*hard!* He hit me so hard that I saw Jupiter, and I saw Mars. That was a lesson for me; that taught me the Messengers were a *group*."

But perhaps the most important lesson learned by Hubbard was to turn himself into a complete musician—and that meant busting out the writing stick. "He gave us a chance to write," Freddie said. "[Pianist] Cedar Walton was writing, Wayne was writing, [trombonist] Curtis Fuller was writing, *everybody* contributed. It was a good opportunity not just to play, but also to get your compositions together. When you're writing for the band, you're creating the sound of the Messengers. You always had to keep that sound going." Keeping the sound going wasn't as difficult as it might seem, because Blakey couldn't help but transform every tune brought in into a Messengers tune. "The way that Art would add his licks and breaks to the compositions I'd write was incredible. The things that he played along with the songs were *right*. He would always play something arousing. He would always put his signature on [the songs]."

"The Core" (*Free for All*, Blue Note, 1964) was one of Hubbard's tunes that got the Blakey treatment. "When I brought in 'The Core,' I wanted it to be a feature to Art. I started teaching him the beat I was looking for that I had copped from [drummer] Elvin Jones. But he played so many polyrhythms against that, he sounded like three drummers. He had his sock drum playing in another meter; each of his hands was doing a different rhythm. It was straight out of the jungle." (That particular album happened to be one of Freddie's personal faves: "Rudy Van Gelder's studio is probably still ringing from *Free for All*.")

Though Shorter's tunes still made up the bulk of the book, Hubbard's pseudo-populist originals gave the band a wider range of colors to draw from. Like Morgan, Freddie was exceedingly at ease writing in 3/4 time: The title cut of *Kyoto* (Original Jazz Classics, 1964) features a swaying melody built dynamically up and down over an extended A-A-B-A format (also, note the coolly dissonant Bud Powell–ish intro); and the tranquil "Up Jumped Spring" (*Three Blind Mice*) was such an amiable ditty that it ultimately became a contemporary jazz standard.

Pretty waltzes aside, Hubbard could also crank out the burners, the most frightening of which was "Thermo" (Caravan). The syncopated intro and the first six bars of the "A" section are straight-up, no-frills hard bop; the triplet run that makes up the final two bars of the "A" section is—to echo Valery Ponomarev—ridiculous. The fact that Hubbard was able to commit such a sharply accented register-jumping line to paper was in and of itself extraordinary; the fact that he could play it with absolute élan was extra-extraordinary.

Many of the second- and third-generation Messengers believed Freddie Hubbard to be the most significant Blakey-ite. Chuck Mangione was blown away from the get-go. "The first time I heard Freddie was at Birdland. I thought it was Sonny Rollins playing the trumpet. He had it all: the chops, the warmth, and a different direction than anybody else who'd played with the band."

"Freddie was an essential idol of mine, one of the most perfect players in the history of the music," Brian Lynch said. Lynch put Hubbard's clout in an historical context by citing Freddie's influence on the picky acolytes of the cerebral, distinctly non-hard-bopping pianist Lennie Tristano. "When you talk to the Tristano-ites, they had their seven or eight players in their canon who they thought you should study and transcribe their solos, such as Bird, Lester Young, Billie Holiday, Bud Powell, Fats Navarro. Towards the end of Lennie's life, he expanded his canon to include Freddie Hubbard. People whose concerns were skewed towards the whole elegance of melody and the treatment of harmony thought that Freddie was tops." In Lynch's mind, Tristano's seemingly against-the-grain adoration of Hubbard made perfect sense. "Somebody who's *really* playing, all of their notes are accounted for—there are no notes flying off in funny directions. Freddie could always start a melodic notion, then not only complete it, but also go to all these different places. As many notes as he played, he didn't waste anything; as much as he can fill up a bar, there's a reason for *all* of those notes." But Lynch did offer up a qualification: "Along with that quality, Freddie has all that fire and emotiveness in his playing—maybe qualities that the Tristano-ites didn't appreciate."

Alto saxophonist Donald Harrison is one of the countless non-trumpeters who were touched by Hubbard. "Freddie is one of *the* guys. I definitely transcribed some Freddie solos [when I was younger]. The way he can swing, the way he can just take over a band, he makes you forget everybody else. I've never heard anything like that. He's got the heart, he's got the mind, he's got the soul, and he's got the chops." Harrison counted himself fortunate to have experienced Hubbard's musical sorcery firsthand. "One time Freddie came and sat in with the band. At that time, Freddie was just leagues ahead of everybody. It was the first time I had heard Art and Freddie play together, and it was just at such a high level." Though intimidated by Hubbard's high level, Harrison took something away from that evening. "I was the last soloist [on one tune], and I was trying to creep into the corner, because Freddie and Art were playing so much music. Art was watching me, and [after the set] he called me over and said, 'Freddie Hubbard. Charlie Parker. John Coltrane. Donald Harrison. Do what *you* gotta do. Get up there and play.' From that point on, I'd just get up there, do the best I could do, then get out of the way."

Pianist Geoffrey Keezer, who was also on that gig, was equally awed. "Freddie came and sat in with the band in L.A., and he was fantastic. It was 1989, and he was in top form. That was the loudest I ever heard Art play; I think he wanted to kick Freddie's ass."

Blakey may have wanted to kick his ass musically, but Art and Freddie's mutual admiration endured for decades. In 1979, fifteen years after Hubbard had left the band, Art Blakey said, "Freddie's so fantastic. I really believe in my heart, about Freddie, that he loved me like he would his father. I really love that man."

Hubbard not only loved Buhaina, but he loved and understood the entire idea of the Jazz Messengers. "I'm so proud of Wynton Marsalis, and Terence Blanchard, and Wallace Roney, and all the young cats. I'm so proud that they're carrying on this music."

FEELIN' GOOD
Chuck Mangione

"When Chuck Mangione was playing with Art, you can definitely hear a trumpet player coming out of the tradition."

—Brian Lynch

YET ANOTHER baseball anecdote, this one courtesy of Chuck Mangione: "As a kid, I was in love with baseball and music. If you were a ballplayer, you wanted to play center field for the New York Yankees. If you were a jazz trumpet player, the gig you wanted to have was with Art Blakey. My dream was to play with the Yankees during the day, and with Art at night."

Sadly, the Yankees thing didn't pan out. Mr. Mantle had center field pretty well sewn up during what would have been Mangione's baseball prime, but thanks to some perseverance and some pasta—that's right, folks, *pasta*— the Rochester, New York, native achieved one of his two life goals.

Chuck became enamored with jazz in general, and Blakey in particular, early in life thanks to his music-loving father. "The first time I saw Art, I was about thirteen years old; the two trumpeters I remember seeing were Kenny Dorham and Bill Hardman. In the early 1950s, when I was a teenager in Rochester, my dad would take my brother [pianist] Gap and I to Sunday afternoon matinees to hear all the jazz bands that came through town. The groups that worked their way across the country would usually start in Albany, then go to Syracuse, then go to Rochester; they'd spend a week or two in each town. When we would go by the matinees, my father would walk up to somebody like Art Blakey and say, 'These are my sons. They can play.' Then we'd get to sit in."

Here's where the pasta comes in. "My dad would then invite the musicians over to the house for spaghetti and Italian wine. One time, Art Blakey came to the house for dinner with the cats in his band." Both the meal and the promising trumpeter captivated Buhaina, so much so that three years later, he made a return trip to Chez Mangione. "I was about sixteen the second time when he came to town, and he asked me to move to New York with him." Though flattered and pleased with the offer, the levelheaded teenager said thanks, but no thanks. "After having seen so many musicians who were kind of scuffling and not really loving being on the road for so many months out of the year, I decided I would complete my education before I did anything like that."

Mangione indeed finished his traditional schooling, but his musical education had just begun. His first high-profile teacher? One John Birks Gillespie. "I'd met Dizzy the same way I met Art, and I fell in love with him because he was a brilliant trumpet player, a brilliant composer who worked with both small groups and large ensembles. I loved his ability to tell the people in the band how to draw the audience in and make them feel very comfortable listening to some very complicated music. I consider Dizzy to be my musical father."

Dizzy wasn't just Chuck's jazz guru, he was also his musical headhunter. "It was 1965, and I had been in New York, trying to get off the ground by free-lancing with different musicians, and I happened to be home in Rochester for my brother's wedding. The phone rang, and it was Art. Dizzy had said to him, 'Do you remember that kid from Rochester?' That's how I got the call."

Chuck wasn't even settled into the Messengers frying pan when Art threw him into the fire. "My first gig was on the Jazzmobile in Harlem. I can't say if I was totally comfortable; there hadn't been much rehearsal. But getting the gig and climbing up on the bandstand was exciting and terrifying at the same time. I can't say I was a novice—I'd already recorded four albums with [my band with Gap], the Jazz Brothers—but this was my first time hard-core touring. This was a whole different kind of experience; I'd never been a sideman for any long period of time, I'd been mostly working in groups with my brother, or things I had put together."

There's scant recorded documentation of the Mangione-era Messengers, but 1966's *Buttercorn Lady*, their lone commercially released session (reissued as *Get the Message*, Drive Archive, 1998) exhibits an ensemble both inside and outside the Messengers tradition. The quintet tackles three of Chuck's compositions—the calypso-bopping "Buttercorn Lady," the 6/8 minor-keyed "Recuerdo," and the modal burner "Between Races"—all of which would fit easily in the Messengers book, be it circa 1960 or circa 1980. (Like many of the band's writers, Chuck was impressed and delighted with Blakey's ability to Messenger-ize any and every composition: "It was always fun to hear the spin that Art put on your music.") As for his playing, Mangione was a lively hornman, his solos bubbly and enchantingly ahead of the beat. His Harmon-muted spot on the brisk rundown of "Secret Love" is a Gillespie-influenced gem, jaunty and self-assured.

While Wynton Marsalis dug Mangione's Messengers work, he felt that Chuck was a perpetuator rather than an innovator. "Chuck's playing was really low-key—it wasn't a step forward, but it wasn't a step backward. Art Blakey's sound was the sound of the Messengers—different people come and go, and they all play differently, but the sound and the feel of the band remained the same. As long as Art was there, that sound would continue. It's like the Boston Celtics with Bill Russell—as long as he was there, you knew the Celtics were going to win the championship."

In light of his eventual career path, it's pretty darn odd to think that Chuck Mangione was once a Jazz Messenger. This isn't to disparage Mangione's wildly popular pop-inflected jazz-fusion recordings, by any means; on the contrary, "Feels So Good" and "Chase the Clouds Away"—two of the trumpeter/fluegelhornist's best-known tunes—are thick with the qualities that make jazz of any sort so alluring: sophisticated melodicism; crescendoing and decrescendoing and re-crescendoing peaks and valleys; and emotion conveyed without words. At the most basic level, there are all the qualities that were atavistic to the Jazz Messengers. Brian Lynch believed that Mangione's experience with Blakey is why his post-Messengers music works so well. "Chuck comes out of the jazz tradition—he's a very smooth, very assured player—but he chose to go in the direction of popularizing the music. He's managed to still keep the jazz spirit alive in his music. He certainly was worthy of being a Messenger, no matter what you think of what he did after that."

Mangione's Messengers weren't as celebrated as the Morgan and Hubbard bands, but, as Wynton said, they still took home a championship trophy, something that Mangione cherishes. "I loved the respect he had for me. I pinch myself every once in a while when I think that I was a part of this company. Part of the reason he's a legend is that he would nurture young musicians, then tell them, 'Go fly on your own.'"

Chuck Mangione heeded Art Blakey's advice, which is part of the reason that for many decades after his Jazz Messengers schooling, Chuck Mangione flew almost as high as any jazz-based instrumentalist has ever flown.

THE SHAW OF NEWARK
Woody Shaw

"Like gold or any precious metal, there's one ingredient that makes it precious. You take that precious thing out, and it becomes just metal. Woody Shaw was that precious thing."

—Valery Ponomarev

WOODY SHAW spent approximately eight months with the Jazz Messengers.

Woody Shaw played on only two Jazz Messengers records.

So considering he was in and out of the band in a flash, why was Woody Shaw such a huge influence on a flock of future Messengers trumpet mavens?

Because, well, he was Woody Shaw. And Woody Shaw had game.

The North Carolina–born, New Jersey–bred hornman had already made a goodly amount of noise before he became a full-time Blakey acolyte in 1972, having apprenticed with Messengers cofounder Horace Silver and Blakey contemporary, drummer Max Roach. A seasoned pro by his mid-twenties, Shaw had an ahead-of-its-time style that was more or less established when he hooked up with Buhaina; it was ultra-distinctive, and virtually without precedent in the band.

Freddie Hubbard believed that Shaw's immediately identifiable sound was rooted in the atypical manner in which he leapt from note to note, from register to register. "He played intervals that made him sound different from *anybody*. He called his style 'intervallic playing.' He was one of the most modern trumpeters of his era." Such modernity was demonstrated in 1973 on Shaw's backbeat-bossa original "Love: For the One You Can't Have." (*Mission Eternal*, Prestige, 1995) The tune's loping tempo gives Woody the opportunity not only to hop around the horn with the greatest of ease, but to kick into double time—and even doubling up, he still bounces from interval to interval, again with a conviction that made his complex lines seem effortless.

Brian Lynch pointed out why so few trumpeters have attempted to draw from Shaw's well of ideas. "What Woody played was really hard, and there was a certain amount of idiosyncraticness to [his playing]. His conception had a lot of things that were worked out a little bit differently than other trumpet players worked things out. It takes a little extra effort to make your sound go around wider intervals on the trumpet; that's why it's hard to make that the core of your style. You have to work at it. He was making progressions that were different, whether it was through a complex tune or a modal sort of thing. There were a lot of things Woody did that trumpeters have yet to explore all the implications of."

Lynch felt that Shaw had a direct, fundamental effect on future Messengers. "You'll hear Wynton Marsalis playing some of his things, you'll hear Terence Blanchard playing some of his things. Those were some of the guys who have explored a little bit more of his playing, some of that intervallic style." Brian spoke the truth: Shaw's spot on the 1972 recording of Cedar Walton's "Anthenagin" (*Child's Dance*, Prestige, 1995) is loaded with the sort of greasy glissandos, punchy trills, and harmonic jumps that Wynton and Terence—either consciously or subconsciously—incorporated into many of their Messenger-era improvs.

In spite of the fact that Shaw's methodology was markedly non-hard-boppish, Hubbard still felt that Woody was fated to become a Messenger, if only because of his attention to history. "Who was Woody Shaw's biggest influence? Lee Morgan. Woody also always wanted to be like me—super hip. Next to me, I would say he was the hippest player of the era."

Lynch was on the same page as Hubbard. "The one thing I've always admired about Art was that he never looked for cookie-cutter players. He was trying to find the best musicians around. Woody was an extension of John Coltrane—he brought a different harmonic sense to the group. It fit in its own way; it was another style for the band."

Trane-isms abounded in the trumpeter's energetic playing, but it was a Coltrane cohort—and the original intervallic jazzer—who ultimately left the deepest impression on Shaw. "One of Woody's biggest influences was [multi-reedist] Eric Dolphy," Lynch said. Hubbard noted, "Woody and Dolphy worked together, and I guess some of that rubbed off on him." So in a sense, Shaw's early gigs helped mold him into the player he was during his Messengers residency. Mathematically, you could break it down along the lines of: Horace Silver's Funk-Bop + Eric Dolphy's Avant-Bop = Woody Shaw.

His stint was brief, but Shaw's effect on Messengers trumpeters was pervasive, if only due to his sheer uniqueness. Lynch nicely summed up Woody's significance, saying, "Woody Shaw was the last innovator in the trumpet lineage."

But Hubbard summed it up even better:

"Woody was *bad*."

MESSENGER FROM RUSSIA
Valery Ponomarev

"Valery Ponomarev was always cool."

—Terence Blanchard

WHEN SOME people think "Russia," they think "Kremlin," or "Red Square," or "harsh winters."

They usually don't think "hard bop badness."

That is, until they dig on Valery Ponomarev.

Born in Moscow, the ambitious trumpet-toter defected to the United States in 1973, carrying with him an abiding love for jazz's preeminent hard bop collective. "The Jazz Messengers sound was the sound that moved me out of the Soviet Union," Ponomarev said.

Valery's spiritual connection with Blakey's music was so powerful that it was only a matter of time before the émigré connected with the educator. "About half a year after I got to the U.S., [the Messengers] were playing at the Five Spot in New York. I went down there and somebody introduced me to Art and told him that I was a trumpet player from Russia. He said, 'Yeah man, bring your horn.' He always welcomed new musicians. So I brought my horn, I played a tune, and he seemed to like me. The trumpeter in the band at that time, Bill Hardman, told me that Art was shocked out of his mind when he heard me play. When I stepped off of the bandstand that night, Art hugged me so hard, I couldn't break away from him. He was like an athlete when he played drums—he sweated like a boxer—and when he hugged me, my new shirt got covered with his sweat and was totally ruined. Art was so open-hearted, so warmhearted, you felt at home right away and I felt I was at home. He told me, 'You'll be playing with my band.'" Blakey's prophecy turned out to be on point. "He took my number, and when Bill Hardman left, he called me and I took his place."

As Ponomarev possessed the fire and funk indigenous to all Messengers trumpeters, he fit into the group from the get-go. "Valery comes straight out of the lineage of Lee Morgan and Clifford Brown," Wynton Marsalis said. "He just has a big heart, both as a person and as a player."

"When I first heard Valery, I kind of thought he was coming out of Clifford," Brian Lynch said, "but he was also listening to Bill Hardman. He has some of that elliptical quality. He's a very fine trumpet player. He swung, he was playing the language, and he was able to tackle the different material that that band was playing with aplomb."

Valery's Clifford-ness caught the ear of the jazz cognoscenti, but he soon found himself pigeonholed, not musically but culturally. "After Art hired me, a lot of people—agents, fans, everybody—asked Art why he had a Russian in the band. Blakey would say, 'Don't tell me who should play in my band.'"

Terence Blanchard, who was first exposed to the Jazz Messengers when Ponomarev was holding down the trumpet chair, also noticed the scrutiny. "One of the things I felt sorry for Valery about was that most people thought of him only as 'The Russian Trumpet Player.' I saw him on the cover of *DownBeat* when I was in high school, and it was touting him as being from Russia, and I was thinking, 'Damn, the man can play, why don't you focus on that?'"

Blanchard was right—the man *can* play. Like most Messengers, Ponomarev thrived in a live setting; each and every one of his solos on the 1978 in-concert session *In This Korner* (Concord Records) are winners. The "I Got Rhythm"-based title cut features Valery Harmon-muting his way through three choruses, a solo that's impressive and notable if only because he manages to utilize the mute without directly aping monster mute-meisters Dizzy Gillespie and Miles Davis. On the Ponomarev-penned blues shuffle "Blues for Two," Valery proudly wears his Clifford influence on his sleeve; the double-time runs, the amiable deconstruction of the blues changes, and the joyful noise all smack of Brownie.

Valery stayed with the Messengers for four years, and might have stuck around several more if it weren't for family obligations. "My ex-wife was having a baby, and I couldn't travel. As much as I hated it, I had to get off the road."

His legacy with the band was based in part on his innate positivity. "I have the utmost of respect for Valery," Wynton said. "I mean, I was young and ambitious, and I came around the band trying to get his job. It was a strange situation. But it wasn't strange to me then, because I didn't know—I was young. But Valery was always very nice to me, always very supportive. He was great as a man."

While many Messengers describe their time with Blakey as "life-changing," few can claim that their lives were as altered as Ponomarev's. And though quite proud of his work with the group, Valery was quick to admit that his edition, while right in the hard-bopping Messengers tradition, wasn't a groundbreaking ensemble. "I can't put the band I was in on the same level as the bands with Lee Morgan or Freddie Hubbard. But it was still the Messengers—the element was still there, no matter who played."

STRAIGHT AHEAD
Wynton Marsalis

"Wynton Marsalis played the most trumpet of any young cat I've ever heard, before or since."

—Charles Fambrough

HE HAD THE CHOPS, he had the tone, he had the roots, he had the swing, he had the smarts, he had the suits, and he had the attitude.

He was Wynton Marsalis, and in 1981, Wynton Marsalis was jazz's mack daddy.

"Wynton hit the scene with the same kind of energy that Freddie Hubbard hit the scene with," said fellow New Orleans brassman Terence Blanchard. "Just like that, Wynton breathed new life into the jazz arena. He was this young guy who could really play the trumpet. When he entered the band, Wynton had a technical prowess that really raised the bar. That was his major contribution."

Brian Lynch echoed Blanchard's sentiment almost verbatim. "When I first heard Wynton, I was astounded. I was blown away. I sat in with the Jazz Messengers around that time, and I thought I had a little something going on [musically], and I was trying to maybe see if I could make a little play [to join the band]. But when I heard Wynton, it was a little dispiriting. He was playing fantastically in that band. He raised the bar so much in terms of technique on the instrument."

According to Chuck Mangione, Marsalis was the total package, not just a fantastic trumpeter, but also a fantastic all-around musician. "When Wynton joined Art, he revitalized the Jazz Messengers. The stamp that he's put on everything he's done came to the front, even at that point. With every edition, you could pick out the musician who was the center of the group—like Horace Silver, or Wayne Shorter, people who took the music in a certain direction. Wynton certainly did that."

Lynch felt that Wynton Marsalis was right in the Messengers tradition. "If Freddie Hubbard was the cutting edge in 1962, and Woody Shaw was the cutting edge in 1973, then you definitely have Wynton Marsalis being the cutting edge in the early 1980s."

Freddie Hubbard believed that Wynton's recipe for musical and critical success was a simple one. "He can play the trumpet because he studies the trumpet. No matter what he plays, he sounds good."

Marsalis was a damp-behind-the-ears seventeen-year-old when he relocated from Louisiana to New York and began to chart out the course of his career. "My roommate [drummer] Akira Tana and I always talked about what it was going to take to learn how to play," Marsalis explained. "Akira said, 'The only chance you'll *really* learn how to play is if you get with Horace Silver or Art Blakey.' Since Horace wasn't working that much, it had to be Art. One night, the band was playing in New York, so I went to the gig and talked to [pianist] James Williams and asked him if I could sit in. And that's what I did."

Right from jump street, Valery Ponomarev—the man Wynton would ultimately replace—gleaned that Marsalis was an enormously gifted cat. "We were playing at Mikell's, and James Williams pointed out this guy and said, 'You ought to talk to him. He's from New Orleans, and he's very young, and maybe you can help him.' So I go over to his table, and see this studious-looking kid. He started talking about trumpet, and it amazed me how much he knew about the instrument. He said, 'I don't really want to play jazz. I want to be a classical musician and play with a symphony orchestra. I want to wear suits and bow ties. I want to travel first class.'" (Marsalis disputes his alleged statements regarding his classical aspirations, saying, "I came to New York to learn how to play jazz.")

Ponomarev was intrigued by the teenage trumpeter's bravado. "I was very curious to hear him play, so I went up to Art and said, 'There's this guy here who you should invite up to sit in.' When Wynton got on the stand, we played [Benny Golson's Messengers standard] 'Along Came Betty.' That song has some tricky chord changes, and if you don't know them, it's difficult to play by ear—you'll get lost. Wynton didn't really know the changes, but even though he was just dancing around the chords, I could tell right away that he could really play the trumpet. The next tune was [another Benny Golson Messengers standard] 'Blues March,' and boy, he blew his ass off on that one. He played so strong, and his tone was great. He blew my mind."

Ponomarev's mind may have been blown, but Wynton wasn't particularly impressed with his own performance. "When I first sat in with [Blakey], I knew I wasn't playing nothing. He said, 'Man, you sad *[sic]*. But that's alright.' And when you were around him, you were around the essence of jazz music. So he put that in us. He said, 'If you want to play this music, you have to play it with soul, with intensity, and every time you touch your horn, you *play* your horn. You know, this is not a game.'"

Marsalis was eighteen when he joined the band in 1980, and nineteen when he departed to launch what would ultimately become one of the most intriguing solo careers in jazz history, a career that ran the gamut from Miles Davis–ish neo-bop to Louis Armstrong–style swing. That said, Wynton was contemplative and a bit wistful about his somewhat abrupt exit from the Messengers. "I probably would have been a different player had I stayed with the band any longer," Wynton said. "It's like any experience you have—everything changes you in some way. Like if you stay with your old lady that you broke up with five or six months longer, it'd change you." Nonetheless, during his ephemeral tenure, he still managed to pick up a lesson or three not just from Buhaina, but also from his fellow Messengers. "Playing with guys like James Williams, and [tenor saxophonist] Billy Pierce, and [bassist] Charles Fambrough, you can't help but learn. They taught me how to play over chord changes, they taught me how to be professional, they taught me to listen to more music, and they taught me how to learn from older people who knew about the music."

Another pearl of wisdom that Marsalis's veteran bandmates divulged was the need to vigilantly study past Blakey-ites. "I remember James would always tell me that I needed to learn more of the Messengers' music. I didn't really know much of the Messengers' music when I was in the band. When I left, I was a little more well versed, but not as much as I should've been."

Blanchard believed that Marsalis was more versed than he let on. "You listen to Wynton in the band, and you can tell he was influenced by Freddie Hubbard. He's not going to admit that, though. He would die and go to his grave before he'd give Freddie credit for being an influence." (Even Hubbard noticed Marsalis's Hubbard-isms. "Wynton would come by my gigs and study all my shit," Freddie said. "One time he sat in with me and played all my licks right back at me.")

Terence may have had a point. The in-concert burner *Art Blakey Is Jazz* (Music Club, 1980) is one of Wynton's earliest recordings with the band, and features a rendition of "Moanin'" in which Marsalis kicks off his solo with that infamous Lee Morgan lick: *Beep bwop boo-da.* But Marsalis claims that

that was merely happenstance. "At the time, I didn't know Lee's solo on 'Moanin'.' I didn't know where that lick was from—I just thought that's how they'd play it in a funk band or something."

The constant gigging with Blakey accelerated Wynton's development to the point that by the time 1981 rolled around, the trumpeter was effectively drenched in Messengers (and jazz) history. His brief but powerful spot on the Wayne Shorter classic "One by One" (*Album of the Year*, Timeless Records, 1981) offers a glimpse of what would ultimately become his personal sound, his brawny and brainy lines evoking the twin specters of Freddie Hubbard and Woody Shaw. By the time 1982 rolled around, Wynton was asserting himself not just as a player, but also as a composer. The minor-keyed "Waterfalls" (*Keystone 3*, Concord Records, 1982) is an altered blues in 6/8 time that, while distinctly Marsalis-ian, could well have come from the pen of Mr. Shorter himself.

In the end, his plunge into the Messengers sea all but made Marsalis the musician he became. "[Playing with Blakey] gave me the opportunity to work and to learn how to play on the bandstand with a master of swing. At the time, there wasn't much swinging going on, so I learned a lot about integrity and belief in something—Art Blakey believed in the music, and he would defend it. There was a feeling around [the music world] that it was a crime for people to try and play [jazz]. Some of that feeling still lingers out there, like you have to apologize for swinging. But Art was unapologetic. If I hadn't played with Art Blakey, I wouldn't have played jazz."

Well, then, we should all get on our knees and thank the jazz gods that Wynton Marsalis played with Art Blakey.

THE HEART SPEAKS
Terence Blanchard

"Terence Blanchard is an astute trumpeter. He's one of the guys that studies."

—Freddie Hubbard

TERENCE BLANCHARD believed himself to be a musical blank slate when he hooked up with Art Blakey and the Jazz Messengers in 1982. "I was nineteen when I joined the band. Was my style developed? Shit, I was still developing pubic hair." Fortunately, during his four-year tenure—one that could be listed in the *Guinness Book of World Records* as "Longest Continuous Stint by a Messengers Trumpeter"—Terence developed a style that, in many ways, was the culmination of the band's trumpet lineage. (At some point during his tour of duty with Buhaina, Blanchard also sprouted some pubes. Whether that had anything to do with his being a Jazz Messenger is unknown.)

Blanchard was attending Rutgers University and gigging with vibraphone legend Lionel Hampton when Wynton Marsalis started talking up his New Orleans homey to Blakey. "When I was leaving, it was either Terence or Wallace Roney who was going to replace me," Wynton said. Though it wasn't his decision to make, the departing Marsalis was secretly rooting for Blanchard to win the trumpet chair. "Wallace would sit in sometimes, and Terence would sit in sometimes. Eventually, Buhaina chose Terence. I knew Terence would bring a soulful thing to the band."

A Messenger audition was generally a high-pressure affair, but Terence was bemused by his tryout. "Donald Harrison came down from Boston, and we were going to learn a bunch of tunes from a list that Wynton had given us. It was pretty funny, because Wynton said, 'Learn these tunes, so when you come and sit in with the band, you'll know that material.' Then we got to the gig, and Wynton asked, 'What tunes did you guys learn?' We told him, then, for some reason, Art called all the tunes we'd learned in the first set while the regular band was playing. So when we got up there to play the next set, we had to repeat all of those tunes. It was funny. The next day, we came back for a rehearsal and auditioned, and I got picked. I was scared to death."

As Wynton had been receiving rave reviews from clued-up jazz heads, fans were somewhat bummed out when they arrived at the club only to see his replacement on the stand. "When we'd hit town, everybody would be expecting Wynton, then they'd be disappointed when I showed up. That whole first year, I went through that shit." In the beginning, even club owners dissed the newcomer. "At my first gig, the first thing that [Chicago's Jazz Showcase proprietor] Joe Segal told me was, 'Don't blow out my microphone. Wynton blew out one of my mikes.'" Terence scoffed at the notion, explaining, "The thing is, that was physically impossible. His mike was old and burnt-out." If anything, this intense scrutiny fueled Terence's desire to tear the roof off the mutha. "You knew who came in the band before you, so you didn't want anybody coming to the shows and saying, 'Damn, he's sad.'"

Blakey used his entire arsenal of teaching techniques to ensure that Blanchard wouldn't be "sad." "When I was first with the band, I told Art, 'I've gotta work on my endurance and chops.' He said, 'Don't worry. I'll get your chops together for you.'" (Freddie Hubbard believed Blakey did indeed lead Terence to the technical Promised Land. "He went through the same shit that I went through: He played too hard, he was overblowing. But Art cooled him out.")

Buhaina also gave Terence a history lesson or three. "I had to go back and listen to all my records. Prior to playing with Art Blakey, all of my jazz heroes were mythic gods. They had reached levels that for me, I thought, were unattainable. When I joined the band, I got the chance to hear Art play the things I'd heard him play on record; I saw how he approached learning tunes, how he approached setting up solos, how he functioned musically. And that made me go back and listen to all those records. I started to see a practical approach to what he was doing, and it started to make everything very real, and very human, and attainable for me. That's one thing he would always talk to me about. He'd say, 'Look, man, Rome wasn't built in a day. You gotta work on this, you gotta work on that.' He'd talk to me about how Clifford Brown could comp for himself when he played a ballad. Things like that were very helpful for me.

"Being in that band confirmed a lot of things that I thought about when I was growing up," Blanchard continued. "Growing up in New Orleans, growing up in the church, I kept hearing how devilish jazz was, and how ruthless the musicians were. To me, that seemed impossible, given how beautiful the music is. I just could never understand how the musicians could be mean—or devil worshipers—and play such beautiful music. So when I started to meet musicians through Art Blakey—and being around him as well … I mean, here's a guy who used to quote the Koran in Arabic. These musicians were searching for truth, and a lot of people couldn't really handle that. That was one of the things that I learned—that these guys were very spiritual, very passionate, very peaceful people."

At the outset, many felt that Terence's primary influence was Wynton Marsalis, a fact that Brian Lynch believes isn't off-base or coincidental. "Terence and Wynton had the same trumpet teacher, Professor William Fielder, who helped them develop those utterly unbelievably gorgeous sounds they both have; also the flexibility and ability to play *through* the horn. When you get to a certain level on the trumpet, things become more possible, like interval jumps or register leaps. It's a technical challenge, especially on the trumpet, but it's also a conceptual thing that you really have to sit down and take some time and *think* about."

Blanchard's mercurial musical growth from Marsalis aspirant to stellar stylist is best exemplified by his performances on two of his original compositions: The May 1984 rendition of his sinewy "Oh, By the Way" (*Coast to Coast*, Concord Records), while undeniably engaging and potent, is semi-derivative—think Wynton on steroids—when compared to his epic rave-up from February 1985's rundown of his distinctly Messenger-ish jam "Two of a Kind." (*Jazz Legends: Live at Ronnie Scott's Club*, BBC Music). Clocking in at five minutes, Terence's built-up-from-the-bottom improv, while oozing originality, is laden with Hubbard's upper-register doubled-up sprints and Woody Shaw's intervallic leaps, qualities that would ultimately become twin cornerstones of Blanchard's mature sound.

Under Blakey's tutelage, Terence developed into not only a musician, but a battle-worn *professional* musician. "That band aged me forty years. It was a love/hate situation, because were having a lot of fun playing with him and being around him, but the touring part of it would take a toll. My first tour of Europe with Art Blakey was a ten-week tour. Suffice it to say that by the end of it, I was fucking tired of Europe. Even with all that, [traveling with Blakey] was the most amazing thing. When we were on the road, we'd hear Art make comments about the things that we would do as young, stupid musicians, and it would get right to the heart of the matter. And he wouldn't even be talking to us—he'd be talking to someone else, and you'd hear him and think, 'Shit, he's right.'"

Blanchard joined the Jazz Messengers a pubeless, hard-blowing trumpet terror, and left the band a pube-laden all-around musician with a distinctive horn sound and a clear-cut musical style. Though his chops and musicality grew by leaps and bounds in his four years with the band, it's possible that the most important lesson he learned was one of humility. "One of the things that people need to know about Art Blakey is what a humble, caring person he was. He would let us call all of the tunes, he wanted us to write the music for the band, and he featured us. That's a very humble thing to do. He'd say, 'I don't want to play drum solos all night. This band is for you guys.'"

SPHERES OF INFLUENCE
Brian Lynch

"Brian was a true Messenger. He did his job as a Messenger perfectly."

—Valery Ponomarev

YOU'D THINK that as the final Jazz Messengers trumpeter, Brian Lynch would blend Freddie Hubbard's musicality, Lee Morgan's funkiness, Kenny Dorham's shrewdness, and Wynton Marsalis's fire. And though Lynch sounded like nobody other than himself, he certainly incorporated stylistic bits and pieces gleaned from his predecessors.

The thing is, he already sounded that way when Bu came callin'. Because unlike 90 percent of the musicians who hooked up with Art Blakey's merry men, Brian Lynch was already a fully realized player when he joined the band.

"Brian Lynch had played with Horace Silver before he was with the Messengers," Terence Blanchard said. "He'd already been out there, and he was an older guy, so when he joined the band, he already had his own thing together. Most of us when we joined the band, we were still kids. That was what the band needed at that time—Philip [Harper] had moved on, Wallace [Roney] was playing with Tony Williams, and I don't know of too many younger guys who were really strong enough to come in at that time."

After earning a Bachelor of Music degree from the Wisconsin Conservatory of Music, the Illinois-born Lynch migrated to New York City, quickly landing gigs with the likes of Eddie Palmieri, Ray Barretto, the Mel Lewis Jazz Orchestra, George Russell's New York Big Band, the Toshiko Akiyoshi Jazz Orchestra, Charlie Haden, Jack McDuff, Phil Woods, and the Frank Wess Quintet.

A veteran when he joined the Messengers in 1988, Lynch, as Blanchard noted, was exactly what the band needed at that time: a knowledgeable, experienced player who could come right in and kick immediate ass at any tempo or dynamic level. His smarts and sensitivity are evident on the standard ballad "I'll Wait and Pray" (*One for All*, A&M, 1990) As with many Messengers ballads, the melody is stated slowly and tenderly, but once the solo kicks in, we're talking big-time double time. After a touching reprise of the melody,

Brian dives into an unaccompanied cadenza that's simply gorgeous, a heartfelt exhibition of sheer musicality that could only come from the lips of a guy who'd been there and done that.

Fiery, consistent trumpeting aside, Brian's compositional work might have been his most important contribution to the Messengers. The band's penultimate album, *Chippin' In* (Timeless Records, 1990), is a showcase for the trumpeter's pen; of the seven originals on the session, three are Lynch's, all of them superb. The album's title cut is a slinky, minor-keyed A-A-B-A groover that, truth be told, feels like it could have been plucked from the Horace Silver songbook. With its oddball form, atypical chord changes, and distinctly Shorter-esque harmonies, the tricky, mid-tempo "Chandek's Den" is also right in the Messengers vein.

But "Byrdflight" is Brian's most original piece, a tune that exhibits what could have been if this edition of the band had had a chance to develop. "'Byrdflight' is dedicated to Donald Byrd," Lynch explained, "and it's based on the chord changes of his composition 'Fly Little Byrd, Fly.' [Tenor saxophonist] Junior Cook introduced me to that song, and he said, 'This is another kind of [John Coltrane's classic] 'Giant Steps.' It has complex chord changes going in a different way; it uses the relationships of minor thirds in the same way that 'Giant Steps' uses the relationship of major thirds."

Whether he knew it or not, Lynch had a big impact on one of his Messenger frontline mates. "Observing Brian," trombonist Steve Davis notes, "I noticed that his sound was always completely opened up. All the obvious things got stronger and stronger. It helped me in the same way, learning how to project."

Taking that into consideration, Brian Lynch was a sphere of influence. A student of the music, he was consciously affected by virtually every Messengers trumpeter, which likely had an unconscious effect on his ability to influence other trumpeters—and, as it so happened, trombonists. So in the end, the music Brian Lynch made was equal to the music Brian Lynch took.

TRUMPET NOTES

WALLACE RONEY was destined to be a Jazz Messenger. "Wallace was very anxious to play with Blakey," Valery Ponomarev said. "We met Wallace when he was in high school in Washington, and he followed us on tour for a while. He had incredible potential, and Blakey helped Wallace Roney realize that potential. After he left the band, he became a superstar. That was what Art Blakey did—create superstars."

Freddie Hubbard also appreciated Roney's individuality. "That boy has one of the most unusual ways of tonguing that I've ever heard." Wallace's spot from his own multifaceted composition "Obsession" (*Feeling Good*, Delos, 1986) confirms that Hubbard was on the money—while out of the University of Miles Davis, Roney's choppy lines and prudently placed slurs are indeed unusual, but his solo is still irrefutably in the Messengers vibe.

One of the things that separated Wallace from his peers was his sense of history. "Wallace knows more about music than almost anybody," Wynton Marsalis said. "Wallace is introverted, but he knows a lot about jazz. He's always very serious about playing."

"One of the most Messenger-ish sounds came out of **Philip Harper**'s trumpet," Valery Ponomarev said. "He was right in the tradition." Indeed Harper, who was with the group from 1987 to 1988, is a Lee Morgan disciple, a warm, churchy player who energized the Messengers' front line.

"Philip was a good fit for the band," Terence Blanchard said. "Philip didn't have a real big sound when he first joined the band, but one thing we kept saying about him was that he could swing, and he could play with the groove. Wynton and I were once talking about him, and we agreed that it was going to take him a while to build up his sound [in a live setting]. We felt that when he makes some studio records, he's going to sound good."

Wynton and Terence were right—he sounded *damn* good on record. His tune "Yang" (*I Get a Kick Out of Bu*, Soul Note, 1987) is a Blue Note–ish Latin-to-hard-bop style-shifter, during which Philip dips into his Lee Morgan bag, trilling and half-valving his way through three choruses.

CHAPTER 3

THE SAXOPHONISTS
Noise in the Attic

"Art played with Charlie Parker, so it was sort of hard for all of us saxophonists to top that."

—Bobby Watson

WHILE VIRTUALLY each and every Jazz Messengers trumpeter was a smack-down fire-breather, the majority of the saxophonists hired by Art Blakey were logicians, jazz intellectuals who could think you into a blissful state of swing-itude.

This isn't to say that the Messengers' reedists couldn't throw it down: During his Messenger years, Benny Golson was, at heart, a cerebralist, but he still had the power to obliterate his typically unobliteratable frontline partner Lee Morgan. It's just that Golson chose to use his power sparingly, making his voyages into the Land of Loud that much more electrifying. And every once in a while, Wayne Shorter—himself a supra-cerebralist—would rear back and go nuclear; his frenetic solo on the title cut of *Free for All* is a picture of straight-up raucousness.

Interestingly, Buhaina's alto saxophonists—i.e., Bobby Watson, Jackie McLean, Donald Harrison—were generally more fiery than the tenorists, and it's interesting because in the Jazz Messengers' storied history, there were only five altoists who had tenures of more than one full year. Compare that to the twenty tenorists who were around for the prescribed twelve months, and you might think that Blakey had issues with the instrument itself. But Harrison didn't feel Blakey held any sort of grudge against the alto—Donald just believed it was a preference issue among modern saxophonists. "For a long time, the tenor was the saxophone of choice. People would always say to me, 'Why're you playing alto?' I'd say to them, 'I'm just playing jazz.' Then they'd ask me why I was playing jazz. When I was in high school, my teacher would tell me and Branford Marsalis, 'Play tenor. Don't play alto.' I just like alto."

Whether by design or happenstance, the Messenger saxists were ideal foils for their brass brethren. And that dichotomy was one of the primary reasons the Jazz Messengers endured longer than your typical hard bop ensemble. If soloist after soloist cranks his volume to eleven, that leaves the band with no place to go dynamically but down. It's true that the hardest of hard bop bands can often deliver exhilarating music, but the Jazz Messengers' wider palette of colors helped raise them to jazz's highest echelon.

STRAIGHT NO FILTER
Hank Mobley

"Hank Mobley was so melodic in everything he played that his solos were like songs unto themselves."

—Bobby Watson

HERE NOW, our final baseball analogy:

One of the highest accolades you can pay a baseballer is to describe him as a "five-tool player." A rare breed, five-toolers can hit for average, they can hit for power, they have speed, they have arm strength, and they can field. Little wonder that those multi-talented athletes are so coveted.

In jazz, five-tool players are equally rare and desirable, and Hank Mobley was a five-tool tenor saxophonist: He had killer chops. He had a silky tone. He could tell the hell out of a story. He was a smokin' composer. And he could swing you into the ground. Five tools. Six, if you count the fact that he looked great on a record cover.

All that said, it's sort of puzzling how Mobley's comparative mellowness worked so well alongside Art Blakey—especially considering that his frontline mate Kenny Dorham, as noted, wasn't exactly a power player himself. The Philadelphia-born Mobley's melodicism united with Dorham's crystalline-sweet-tart-genial allure to create a sound that was *right*, so right that the duo exuded a sense of quiet storm, even when Buhaina got to bashing. Horace Silver opined, "Kenny and Hank were a beautiful front line. They were so compatible. They just happened to click."

Before Blakey recruited Hank in 1954, Mobley spent two years apprenticing in Max Roach's band, thus, by the time he joined the Jazz Messengers, he had already learned how to prosper alongside a domineering drummer. Few of his saxophone-playing peers understood that the contrast of using a smoother, more refined attack next to a bumptious percussionist would make them come off like graceful bebop swans rather than hammer-tongued jazz orcas. Tenorist Javon Jackson was among the many who appreciated Mobley's effect on the Messengers. "What Hank brought to the band was a relaxed feel. He was strongly influenced by Sonny Rollins—a person that I'm influenced by—but like all [post-bop saxophonists], he comes from Charlie Parker. Hank was also a strong melodicist, and Art Blakey loved Hank."

That love was mutual, as evidenced in the way Mobley—and, for that matter, Dorham—played off of Blakey, and vice versa. "Room 608," the very first cut on the very first Jazz Messengers record (*Horace Silver and the Jazz Messengers*), is a twisty-turny Silver composition, a medium/up-tempo jam with a garrulous melody; Mobley and Dorham are almost gentle in their interpretation, two hot 'n' cool hard boppers breathing as one. Hank, the tune's final soloist, slithers and dances around the changes, proving himself to be a natural link between Parker and Rollins.

"[Drummer] Louis Hayes once told me that Hank prided himself on not playing anything corny," Jackson said. "He was a very sophisticated soloist." Only twenty-five at the time of the 1955 *Café Bohemia* sessions, Mobley the saxophonist was already elegant and mature beyond his years—corniness, even at that tender age, wasn't in the equation, even on a hoary old standard like "Alone Together" (*Bohemia, Volume 1*). Utilizing his entire dynamic, harmonic, and rhythmic range, Hank's reading was haunting and resonant, a skillful blend of sensuality and swing.

Mobley's busy pen was cherished both in and out of Jazz Messengers circles. "His writing is among the top in the history of the music," Bobby Watson said. "His tunes were smooth and laid-back, but still intense." (Watson felt Mobley's compositional silkiness stemmed in part from his soulful upbringing: "No doubt, it was a Philly thang.") While Mobley's writing skills didn't fully blossom until the early 1960s, the tunes he dropped into the Messengers' laps dripped with potential. Kicking off with a slick Middle Eastern–flavored intro, the aptly titled "Hank's Symphony" (*Bohemia, Volume 2*) is an intricate Latin modal smoker, a three-movement feature for Blakey with nary a horn or piano solo to be heard; it's almost as if Mobley felt the tune was too precious to be sullied by improvisation. Waxed at the same session, "Avila & Tequila" demonstrates Mobley's ability to personalize a typical jazz formula; utilizing a standard A-A-B-A format, Hank's cycle-of-fifth-rooted chord changes bear nothing in common with the A-A-B-A tunes (e.g., "I Got Rhythm" and "Honeysuckle Rose") upon which many hard bop tunes were based.

Hank briefly rejoined the Messengers in 1959, a stint documented on the two ...*At the Jazz Corner of the World* recordings. In his four years away from the band, Mobley—who, during his time away from Blakey, had garnered heady experience leading his own bands—had honed his sense of refinement, developed a sense of modernity, and bolstered his chops. His lone chorus on Randy Weston's "Hi-Fly" (*Jazz Corner*, Volume 2) is highlighted by a series of Coltrane-esque honks and squeaks that, while raw and harsh, never cause his solo to veer off track.

Because his playing was relatively subtle, one might assume that Hank Mobley had only a small impact on what became the band's overall sound. But the fact of the matter is that Mobley was a distinguished presence that all Messengers tenorists had to acknowledge and deal with if they had any desire to be a true Messengers tenorist.

DR. JACKLE
Jackie McLean

"Jackie McLean was the precursor to an entire generation of altoists."

—Donald Harrison

IT WAS ALL but preordained that Jackie McLean would join forces with Art Blakey.

McLean had learned how to bop at the knee of Charlie Parker. He'd spent his adolescence hanging out with tenorist Sonny Rollins and pianist Walter Davis Jr. He'd cut his teeth professionally with Miles Davis and Charles Mingus. His altoisms always piped with fire and brimstone. He could simultaneously look upon the past and the future, the forward and the backward, the up and the down. And he could swing his *tuchas* off.

So how could he *not* become a Messenger?

"*Everything* Jackie played swung," Bobby Watson said. "He hung out with Bird, so he got it firsthand. He's always been one of my idols, one of my role models on the horn. Him and Sonny and Walter were bebop babies. He was there when the bebop bomb went off. He brings that spirit to everything he does."

Personified by a new-school slant on old-school bop and a hyper manner of steering through the slipperiest of chord changes, that McLean spirit was a vital ingredient in shaping the sound of what could be viewed as the possibly the first "real" edition of the Messengers. Though Jackie's voice was up front in the 1956 assemblage's, particular mix, the altoist gave Buhaina credit for the end product. "I went with Art Blakey, the Daddy, when I left Mingus," he said. "I worked with Art for nearly three years and traveled all over the States. He was the greatest bandleader I've ever worked with—as a leader. He's strong, tenderhearted, firm, and quite intelligent. He set a pace as far as swinging goes, and very few could keep up with him night after night."

McLean believed he couldn't hang with Bu on the bandstand on a nightly basis—a belief that was patently false—but in the studio, he was always right on Blakey's tail, and vice versa. On a 1956 arrangement (or derangement) of "Stella by Starlight," (*Hard Bop/Paris Concert*, BMG Collectables, 1995), Blakey is hard-pressed to match Jackie's vigor on what, at that point, was one of the more lengthy Messenger solos heard on wax. The drummer fares better on the up-tempo "Evans" (*A Night in Tunisia/Play Lerner and Lowe*); McLean, as usual, sprints ahead of the beat, but in this case Art manages to keep pace—more or less.

Like that of Woody Shaw, with whom he'd eventually record, Jackie's style was so singular that few hard bop or post-bop altoists were able to cop his concept. But Donald Harrison—one of the few contemporary saxists who tried to bask in McLean's vibe—didn't think it was McLean's lines or sound that were so significant, but rather the way he viewed the instrument itself. "Jackie was one of the first alto players to really deal with playing sounds that came from the tenor saxophone and other instruments," Harrison said. "He opened up the sense of what the alto could do. He was a brilliant musician, and he could play anything. You put him in any situation, and he knew his way around. He showed that the alto could do more than what people said it could do. He dealt with John Coltrane and Sonny Rollins—and everything he heard—instead of just other alto players. I would bet he also listened to Miles a lot, plus other trumpeters and a lot of pianists; those instruments have a much bigger range than the alto. I try to extend the range like that. I figured, if Jackie could do it, I could do it."

Inspired by Blakey's ability to inspire, McLean himself became a teacher—in 1990, he landed a gig as the artistic director for the Hartt College of Music in Hartford, Connecticut, where he went on to found the Jackie McLean Institute of Jazz. One of his more successful students at Hartt was Steve Davis, possibly the lone jazzer to have sidemanned with both Blakey and McLean. The trombonist was highly gratified to have been taken under the master's wing: "Jackie's sense of the history while simultaneously moving forward with the music is strong. He taught me how to really take care of business on the bandstand, that the bandstand is a sacred place. He taught me to play hard every time, wherever you are, if you're tired, if you're sick, if you're hungry, or if you're depressed. When it was time to play, those [older] guys played like it was the last time—*every time*. [Seeing] that made an impact on me as a young musician, how serious the music is, how powerful the music is, and my responsibility to carry those thoughts into the world, and to develop my own voice. It's definitely fire. Playing with Art, the fire was coming from the drums, but playing with Jackie, I had to stand next to him every night and just try to follow that—talk about humbling. But Jackie had a way of feeding you conviction. I remember one time I was thinking that I wasn't playing well enough, I wasn't playing what I wanted to play, and maybe I cracked some notes. Jackie said, 'If you miss something that you were trying for, man, nobody knows but you.' He gave you this feeling that everything you played when you played with him was special. He instilled a real confidence in me."

Professor McLean was a first-class teacher primarily because he imparted upon his students the lessons that Buhaina imparted upon him. "With Blakey, I had the most wonderful experience being in a band," McLean said. "I learned how to grow up and be a man around Art. He was an incredible individual, and a wonderful bandleader. He had a fatherly role that he played as a bandleader—[for example], if you had a toothache, he took you to the dentist. He looked out for everybody in the band, and he also was very much into bringing young musicians into his band and helping them develop."

Deep down, Blakey knew that J-Mac was, in many ways, irreplaceable, which was probably why he covered up his love for McLean with a joke: "He honored me by telling me that I was the only alto player he would hire," Jackie said, "[but] he's used [other altoists] since." Blakey may have had his tongue planted firmly in his cheek when he proposed his post-Jackie ban on the alto saxophone, but as we all know, behind every joke lays a grain of truth. In other words, Buhaina knew that if an altoist desired to make it as a Messenger, he would be required to possess Jackie McLean's "bebop baby" spirit.

ALONG CAME BENNY
Benny Golson

"Benny Golson is a bad dude."

—Branford Marsalis

"THE THING that people don't give Art Blakey credit for is that he saved jazz," Terence Blanchard said.

Nobody will dispute that. But Art Blakey couldn't have saved jazz if Benny Golson hadn't saved the Jazz Messengers.

It wasn't as if the Philly-born tenorist/composer—who, before he encountered Blakey, was fresh off a stint with the Dizzy Gillespie Big Band—had set out to rescue the Messengers from a sticky situation, nor was it as if Benny had some self-serving master plan to reshape the band's musical and professional style. Everything just sort of happened. "[One day] in 1958, [the phone rang], and it was my hero," Golson said, "Art Blakey was on the phone. [Jackie McLean] was having trouble getting a cabaret card from the police and [Blakey] asked me to come in and sub for a night. 'Oh, my God,' I said to myself. *'Art Blakey!'* He didn't know it, but I would have played for free. And I went down and played, and I noticed that although the band had been together for a while, not much was happening—[they were] just [playing] tunes. But on a personal level, he just laid me out. I'd never played with a drummer like that before."

At the end of that night, Benny was aghast with the Jazz Messengers' paltry paycheck. "I said, 'Art, you're a great man; this pay is nothing for you. It makes me sad.'" Blakey knew Golson's assessment was accurate, so he asked the tenorist for some assistance. "He looked at me with his sad, beautiful cow eyes and said, 'Can you help me?' And I can't believe what came out of my mouth, this young man who hadn't been in New York too long. I said, 'Yes, if you'll do exactly what I tell you.' How dared I? But he went for it. He said 'What should I do?' And I said, 'Get a new band.'"

Enter Benny's homeboys Lee Morgan, pianist Bobby Timmons, and bassist Jymie Merritt. "Benny's band was all Philadelphia people," Javon Jackson said. "That was all orchestrated by Benny." Initially, Buhaina was suspicious about the influx from the City of Brotherly Love. As Golson remembered, "Blakey asked, 'What's all this Philadelphia stuff?' I told him, 'Trust me.'"

So Blakey trusted him. And that trust paid dividends. Immediately.

Only six months after he joined the band, Benny Golson—with the Philly dudes in tow—was the prime creative force behind one of hard bop's greatest albums, *Moanin'*. Again, the fact that he all but led the session wasn't a calculated move on Benny's part—it just happened. "I can't tell you why [they used my ideas]," Golson said, "but everything I suggested, these people were doing. I said, 'The name of this album should be *Moanin'*, and I have a photograph here that a fan took of Art.' It's the headshot on the album."

Golson had not only become the de facto art director, but also the musical director, and as musical director, it was his job to choose the repertoire. Rather than use outside sources, Benny reached within himself and banged out a quartet of killer tunes, two of which remained vital components of the Jazz Messengers songbook up until the very end.

"'Along Came Betty' is one of the most beautiful tunes in jazz history," Valery Ponomarev raved. "It's so emotional, so expressive." Ponomarev doth not exaggerate: A lilting mid-tempo A-A-B-A joint with a two-bar tag, "Betty" is at once singable and unforgettable, which is amazing considering the song's harmonic complexity. The beauty of Golson's one-chorus solo matched the gorgeousness of the melody: After whispering his way through the first sixteen bars, Golson cut loose on the bridge, glissandoing like Ben Webster, bull-in-a-china-shopping like Coleman Hawkins, and boogieing over the changes like Charlie Parker. "When you listen to Benny Golson's solo on 'Along Came Betty,'" said Terence Blanchard, "you realize that that was the perfect sound for that band at that time."

Benny's second soon-to-be classic was a goofy twelve-bar blues-rooted jam that had a peculiar precedent. "[When I wrote] 'Blues March,' I knew it couldn't be the kind of march you hear from military bands," Golson explained. "It had to be a funky, Grambling College–type thing. It's a blues, but just a little different. I figured it was a novelty and would never last, just something to get us over, maybe. I took it in and we rehearsed it. I told Art to pretend he was with the American Legion band, and he did. Until this day, nobody has played 'Blues March' the way Art Blakey did, and I've played it with some of the best jazz drummers in the world."

Though it was a Bobby Timmons composition, Golson's fingerprints were all over the classic title cut. "When they got into the studio," Javon

Jackson said, "Bobby Timmons kept messing with this little eight-bar thing, and Golson said, 'Man, what is that? You need to put a bridge to that!' He did, and then he had 'Moanin'.'"

Benny was correct in assuming that Timmons's tune would be a hit. "When he [first] played it for me, I said, 'That's it. Come on, let's learn it. When we play it tonight, I'm going to pay particular attention to the audience, and they will tell us if there is anything to it at all.' So that night [at the gig], I made an announcement: 'Ladies and gentlemen, this is an original tune. We're going to present it tonight, and we just want to have your reaction to it.' We went into it. There was no dancing [allowed] in the club, [but] man, they were dancing in between the tables and knocking over the chairs."

What made Benny's miniature symphonies so endearing was their sheer freshness. "He wrote tunes that weren't really based on anything," Watson said. "They had a sound of their own. His tunes didn't really draw from any-where—they just stood on their own with the form, and the chord progres-sions, and the chromaticism."

A smash hit with critics and fans alike, *Moanin'* gave the Jazz Messengers the opportunity to take their message not just all over America, but also across the Atlantic. "I called the booking agency and asked why Art hadn't been to Europe," Golson said. "We went to Europe, and they loved him; he could do no wrong. Before *Moanin'*, some places [in the States] did-n't want Art to come back a second time because he had a habit of being a lit-tle late, taking an intermission, and disappearing. So I would just make sure he was there. I would pick him up, go to work, and when it was time to come back from intermission, I'd make everybody come back. One of the major clubs, Small's Paradise—the original one uptown that said they never wanted to see him in their club again—asked him to come back after *Moanin'* came out and was on all the jukeboxes."

(It's worth noting that Golson wasn't just the band's musical guru, but also its sartorial advisor and den mother. "Benny got the band wearing suits," Jackson said. "He made sure they were on time. Before him, the band was raggedy." For his part, Blakey appreciated Golson's punctuality. "Benny could always keep the band in line. He was always on time. We used to call him 'On Time Charlie.'")

Branford Marsalis believed that Golson was an individualist not just as a composer, but also as an improviser. "Benny Golson was underappreciated because of his playing style. His style was fully immersed in the bebop tradition, but he didn't employ bebop licks, which was the standard of the time. People had these ideas and notions about how jazz was supposed to sound, and how tenor players were supposed to sound. When Benny went against that grain, there was a side of him that people didn't really understand. They didn't understand the genius of being able to break away from the mold."

Golson felt that much of his style stemmed from having Blakey lay into him night in and night out. "He was trying to [teach] me without words, with the drums," Benny said. "He'd get the beat going up underneath me. He'd make those press rolls four bars before going into the chorus, getting louder and louder, and I would just disappear, standing there pantomiming. I didn't get it. And one night, he did one of these press rolls, then he did it again. At the beginning of the next chorus, he came down with a crash. Then he played another crash right behind it, then another, as if to say, 'Don't you get it?' And then to underscore all of that, he hollered over to me as I was playing, 'Get up outta that hole!' And I had to start learning to play a little louder and a little more aggressive. That smooth, syrupy stuff wasn't working.

"Art Blakey was a teacher," Golson continued. "He was didactic. He was a teacher and didn't know that he was a teacher. Just by the things that he said, the things that he did, and the way that he played the drums. Just by being with him for just about a year was like being enrolled in a college of higher education. He taught us all things because he had vast experience. He had such a penchant for swinging. He didn't know how not to swing, and that really left a mark on me. So much so that when I left him, I found I had great difficulty in playing with other drummers for a while."

Buhaina was eternally grateful for Golson's contribution to the band. Javon Jackson remembered an instance where Blakey gave the saxophonist the highest possible accolade: "One time when Art was introducing Benny on stage, he said, 'This guy is the reason I'm here now.'"

Deep down, Art Blakey knew he himself had saved jazz. Deep down, Art Blakey knew that Benny Golson saved the Jazz Messengers.

CONTEMPLATION
Wayne Shorter

"If it were up to Art, Wayne Shorter would have been in the band forever."

—Javon Jackson

AS BOTH a saxophonist and composer, Wayne Shorter somehow managed to meld Hank Mobley's five-tooled-ness, Jackie McLean's combustibility, and Benny Golson's rock solidness into a vibe that just about every future Jazz Messenger, regardless of his instrument, endeavored to integrate into his musical personality.

Javon Jackson was one of the many Messengers who genuflected at the altar of Wayne. While he appreciated Shorter's Mobley/McLean/Golson amalgam, Javon believed Wayne's omnipresent effect on the band's sound had to do not just with his attention to the Messengers lineage, but with his sheer individuality. "Wayne was influenced by Sonny Rollins, Trane, Lester Young, Charlie Parker—it's all in there—but it comes out differently. His stuff is so all-encompassing; he was a composer on saxophone. Wayne would play some stuff, and sometimes you wouldn't get it, because he was painting a picture. He was a dynamic figure."

Branford Marsalis pretty much concurred with Jackson's view, but he also felt that Shorter was right out of the Messengers tradition, if only because his thought process echoed that of his immediate predecessor. "Wayne had the same thing that Benny Golson did, that same way of internalizing the history of the music by learning how to play while [listening to] a lot of different guys. He was a master mimic—he could play like Bird, he could play like Lester, he could roll like Coltrane; that's what enabled him to play the way he did, because he had many more reference points than everybody else. Wayne Shorter was the king."

Born in Newark, New Jersey, and educated at New York University, King Wayne was introduced to the music-listening public in 1956 during a brief spell with Horace Silver. A two-year tour of duty in the Army temporarily derailed his burgeoning career, but after fulfilling his military obligation, Shorter promptly picked up where he left off, landing a job with trumpeter Maynard Ferguson's big band—a job that, thanks in part to Lee Morgan, ended on the quick. "We were at [the 1959] Canadian Jazz Festival, and the Jazz Messengers came on," Shorter recalled, "and they had no tenor player. Blakey was playing Monk's tune 'Evidence'—Blakey would say 'We'd like to play a tune by the high priest of bop. He calls it "Evidence," but we call it "Justice"'—and Lee Morgan saw me from the bandstand. After the set he came running over and said, 'Hey, Wayne, you want to play with us?' And I said, '*Shit*, yeah!'"

Initially, the loyal Shorter was concerned about leaving Ferguson in the lurch; but Blakey—in an exceptionally cryptic and charismatic manner—sour-and-sweet-talked both Wayne and Maynard into submission. "[After the set], I went back and saw Art Blakey," Shorter said, "and he said just one sentence: 'You got eyes?' I said yeah, I got eyes." (Say what?) "But I'd only been with Maynard for four weeks and that would've been disloyal [to leave], like hello, goodbye. So later, Maynard gets a call from Art [who was] way down in French Lick, Indiana. 'Look, we're in trouble. We don't have a sax player and you know Wayne ain't gonna stay with you too long because he's a small-group man.'"

Though he'd already obtained a bunch of hands-on professional experience, Shorter disagreed with Buhaina's original assessment, believing himself ill prepared for the small-group solo-intensive setting—but Dr. Blakey had little problem whipping Wayne into shape. "The kind of timing I learned with Art was almost always consistent, building your expressions into sort of a climax, ending your solos on something very worthy of sharing with or being remembered by everyone." (Branford shared a similar experience when he first joined the band: "Benny Golson told me, 'The great thing you're doing is that you're learning how to play like all the cats. Then one day, you'll blossom into yourself.'")

Nobody doubted that Wayne was a font of jazz data, but Blakey opined that the reticent Shorter wasn't immediately able to share his musical insight with the world at large. "[The whole band] spent a lot of time bringing Wayne out of his shell. He has so much knowledge, but we had to bring him out as a tenor player, so he could get out front and play his horn, play what he knew. Because he's very shy. [At first], Lee Morgan's personality and Bobby Timmons's personality overshadowed Wayne so much."

Buhaina's observation was more than a little astute. Shorter's first studio recording with the Messengers was *Africaine* (Blue Note, 1959); his playing throughout is superb, but lacks the sang-froid he would demonstrate even a few months later. On the title cut, for example, the notes are there, but harmony-wise—aside from a nifty double-time run at the top of his second chorus—he keeps his lines well within the constraints of the chord changes. Dynamically, Wayne had yet to master the art of building a solo from the bottom up, and his volume level remains, well, level throughout. (The fact of the matter was, at that point, Lee Morgan was kinda blowing Shorter away.)

His increasingly assured work on the multiple renditions of "Lester Left Town"—a magnificent Shorter composition dedicated to tenor mastermind Lester Young—is a clear display of Wayne's growth as an improviser. "Lester" stayed in the Messengers' book for three of Wayne's five years with the band, and his reading improved with each performance. On the 1959 recording from the aforementioned *Africaine* session, the tempo is comparatively slow—jazzers almost always speed up tunes with repetition—and Shorter's improv, while again superb, is composed mostly of held tones and eighth-note runs, thus lacking the exploratory nature of subsequent recordings. A live performance just two weeks after the studio session (*Live in Stockholm*, Dragon, 1959)—which Blakey introduced by noting the song was "hot off the griddle"—demonstrates how important it can be to have an extra week or three to 'shed on a song; rhythmically, harmonically, and dynamically, Shorter's lines are far more assertive—he doubles up, jumps from register to register, and generally wails like the Wayne he would ultimately become. Five months later, the band cut the definitive studio rendition (*The Big Beat*). Faster-tempoed than any of the previous recordings, it features a Shorter solo that's positively giddy, and unlike the 1959 studio take, it's Shorter who kinda blows Morgan away.

By the time Freddie Hubbard replaced Morgan in 1961, Wayne's playing style—a fusion of brawn, intellectualism, and ingenuity—had been firmly established; thus, Hubbard and the also newly arrived Curtis Fuller, having likely heard the Messengers' many recent recordings, had a sense of what was necessary to fit in alongside the tenorman. The fact that Freddie and Curtis showed up to the shooting range already locked and loaded is the chief reason the 1961–64 Shorter/Hubbard/Fuller band was flawless from the start, one of *the* preeminent—if not the preeminent—Messenger ensembles.

Mosaic was the group's debut, and from note one, it was obvious that this sextet was going to be magical. Shorter's contribution "Children of the Night" fit the band hand in glove—it lopes along at a tempo fast enough to be invigorating, but slow enough to allow for maximum slammage.

"Wayne has a lethal pen," Branford Marsalis said. "That's part of why he was the king. Wayne wrote *compositions*, not *tunes*."

"Horace Silver was the reason that Wayne wrote the way he wrote," Jackson said. And though Shorter's modernized, against-the-grain harmonic and structural concepts had little in common with Silver's blues-based philosophies, their respective tunes did share one vital quality: They were Jazz Messengers tunes. (But as Freddie Hubbard noted, Blakey made every tune sound like a Jazz Messengers tune.)

"Art talked about Wayne as having the imagination of a child," Terence Blanchard said, "and you can hear that in some of his arrangements. One of the things that I love about Wayne is that he had a very strong influence on that band in terms of his arrangements. He made that small group sound like a big band."

"Wayne was my role model, one of my all-time favorite composers," said Bobby Watson, a mean composer himself. "What I take from him is his individuality, the way he could create a mood."

Buhaina revered Shorter's writing skills from the onset. "Art Blakey used my tunes right from the beginning," Shorter said. "[For *A Night in Tunisia*] (Blue Note, 1960), I wrote 'Sakeena's Vision' about his daughter, and 'Sincerely Diana' was about Art's wife. I was getting away from the old twelve-bar structure, you know; the melody can go somewhere else, or come back to itself, but in another way."

From 1962 to 1964, Blakey took a hiatus from recording for the Messengers' longtime label, Blue Note; over that two-year span, the band cut a pair of albums that are among the Messengers' most timeless, if only because of Shorter's small-band sonatas.

Shorter supplied six of the ten originals heard on *Caravan* (Riverside, 1962) and *Ugetsu* (Riverside, 1963), all of which could be placed in a time capsule as models of hard bop perfection: "Sweet 'n' Sour" is a sixteen-bar-with-a-tag waltz, at once funky and knotty. "This Is for Albert"—dedicated, oddly, to Bud Powell, whose birth name was Earl—is supported by a sumptuous set of harmonies and chord changes, concurrently gorgeous and potent. "One by One" was one of the Messengers' "greatest hits," a sweet shuffle that Blakey kept in the repertoire until the end. "Ping Pong" was a neck-bobber whose groovy beat was, in a sense, ahead of its time, as demonstrated by the fact that in the mid-1990s, a handful of acid jazzers and hip-hoppers sampled the song's syncopated piano intro. The festive "On the Ginza" gave Buhaina the opportunity to smack the front line upside their collective head. And finally, the tone poem "Eva" is a Jazz Messengers anomaly; four of the tune's six minutes are devoted to the dense melody, with only a brief Cedar Walton solo to relieve the tension.

Shorter was fertile beyond any composer's wildest dreams—the band recorded at least thirty-five of his tunes over a five-year period, which meant he was cranking out in the neighborhood of three-fifths of a song per month—but according to Javon Jackson, there could well have been more, *much* more. "Curtis Fuller once told me that Wayne was writing two or three songs a week, but most of them he'd throw away."

Shorter loved being a Messenger, and believed that Blakey's leadership gave him the opportunity to spread his wings, which helped prepare him for the next phase of his career. "Before I left, we were starting to stretch out with the arrangements, trying an extended kind of thing with three horns in front on tunes like 'Mosaic' and some of the other things we wrote." Even so, Wayne knew it was time to move on. "At that time I was getting calls from Miles [Davis], so I figured five years, that's enough for a cycle." (In a sense, Davis "stole" Shorter away from the Messengers. "[Miles] called me and said, 'Come to California.' He sent me a first-class ticket and I flew to California. Within a couple of days [the group] walked onstage at the Hollywood Bowl." Losing Shorter to Davis via burglary could have been Blakey's karmic payback for stealing Wayne from Maynard Ferguson in the first place.)

"One thing that was brilliant about Wayne was that he played completely different with Bu than he did with Miles," Branford said. "Blakey was about the show. The first and last songs of every set were going to be, *bang, bang*. Even when you played ballads, the ballads had to have a cadenza at the end—it wasn't about the embodiment of the composition. It was about the show. And Wayne was able to function in any setting by keeping his eye on the larger picture."

Wayne Shorter never received the widespread critical acclaim heaped upon Charlie Parker, Miles Davis, John Coltrane, or Ornette Coleman. But in his own shy way, this "dynamic figure," this artist with "the imagination of a child," this "king," created enough inventive improvisations and compositions to merit a place alongside the greatest of the great.

GLOWING
David Schnitter

"David Schnitter was from Newark, but he had New York oozing out of his pores."

—Bobby Watson

DIG THE first line of Burt Bacharach and Hal David's timeless ballad "A House Is Not a Home":

A chair is still a chair, even when there's no one sitting there.

Now, Burt may not be a bebopper, but that lyric is an apt depiction of the Jazz Messengers' post–Wayne Shorter saxophone situation; after Shorter split, the Messengers tenor chair was a virtual revolving door—but, as the song says, it was still a chair. "[By 1975], *every* chair was pretty much in flux," tenor saxist David Schnitter pointed out. "I don't think he really had a steady band or steady work at that time. But the band was still going."

Yes, the Messengers train was still chugging along—but only barely. In the mid-1970s, hard bop was *way* out of vogue. At the time, the two most visible forms of improvised instrumental music were jazz-rock fusion (think Weather Report, Return to Forever, and Mahavishnu Orchestra) and what is most often referred to as avant-garde (think Art Ensemble of Chicago, Anthony Braxton, and Ornette Coleman.) But Art Blakey was a trooper—he wasn't going to let trends dictate his musical life. Fortunately, there were a handful of simpatico instrumentalists who had Buhaina's back, one of whom was the abovementioned Mr. D. Schnitter.

"In 1974, before I hooked up with Blakey," Schnitter recalled, "I was playing at a club in New Jersey called Boomer's. One night Art came down there and sat in with me—I used to have a lot of musicians sit in with me anyway, but of course I was honored that he played with me. After the set, he said, 'You're gonna be in my band!' He said he'd call me when he was going to start his rehearsals. He eventually called, and I made a gig at the Village Gate."

David needed a whole heap of encouragement from Blakey before he felt comfortable as both a Messenger and a Big Apple-er. "It took me a while to get the courage to come to New York—I was scared. But Art helped give me confidence. Being in the Messenger environment was a growing experience, both musically and personally. The first time I ever went out of [New

Jersey or New York] was when I went with him to Baltimore. The first time I ever went on a plane was when we took a shuttle to Boston."

Once Schnitter became firmly entrenched in the band, Blakey began to use the saxophonist as a sounding board, even when it came to personnel decisions. "Art asked me who I wanted to play with, and I said Bill Hardman, because I wanted to play with a veteran." Hardman—in one of his many return trips—shared the front line with David for two years, a period during which the Messengers slowly rose Phoenix-like from the jazz ashes. "Little by little, we started getting more work," Schnitter said. "At first, we would work a couple of times a month, but pretty soon—after three or four months—it started picking up. For the next six or so months, we were working almost every weekend, somewhere."

At the beginning of 1977, Valery Ponomarev and Bobby Watson joined Schnitter, building the most cohesive horn section the Messengers had seen since the Hubbard/Shorter/Morgan band; and Walter Davis Jr.—in one of *his* many return trips—handled the keys. "Aside from Walter, I was the veteran of that band," David noted. But it was when James Williams replaced Davis that things began to turn around. "That band was tight, and it kept getting tighter and tighter."

That tightness is exemplified by the band's ability to nail even the most demanding ensemble passages. Full of stops, starts, dense harmonies, and technically challenging lines, Walter Davis's hyper-tempoed "Jody" (*In My Prime 1*, Timeless Records, 1978) is one of the most difficult—and most enduring—songs to grace the band's book. Cohered by the "veteran" Schnitter, the horns eat up both the melody and its subsequent in-between-solos interludes. And Schnitter's solo is a wonderful example of his ability to accelerate from zero to sixty over the span of two mere choruses.

According to Bobby Watson, Schnitter was, in many ways, the band's heart and soul. "David influenced me with his experience," Bobby Watson said. "When I got into the band, he'd already been there for three years. I looked up to David a lot in terms of how to be a professional, in terms of the consistency of his playing. I watched how he lived on the road; I learned a lot from him."

The reason David Schnitter was such a fine teacher? Because he was an equally fine student. "I was on the road all the time," he said. "I saw the world—that was an education. Playing every night will help a person grow musically. Playing with Art, watching him, you can't help but grow. He used to say the Messengers builds men, just like the Marines."

All of which is why that chair was always still the chair.

IN CASE YOU MISSED IT
Bobby Watson

"Both musically and charismatically, Bobby Watson was a truly dominant presence in the Jazz Messengers."

—Branford Marsalis

"THE JAZZ MESSENGER resurgence started when me, David Schnitter, and Valery Ponomarev came together," Bobby Watson said. That's when the band started getting good gigs. That group started to develop a reputation, and people who had stopped coming to hear the Messengers started coming back."

It's no coincidence that people started coming back at that point. After all, Watson, who was the group's musical director, was one of the most musically charismatic chaps ever to share the stage with Art Blakey. A hyperdynamic alto saxophonist, Watson was one of only three reedists to spend at least four years in the band.

Watson had absorbed the Messengers' musical concept during his formative years, but he didn't learn what they were truly about until he'd entered Buhaina's sphere. "I'd always dug the band," Bobby said. "I loved *Free for All, Mosaic, Ugetsu*—I used to listen to them in college. I used to wake up to *Free for All* every morning. But I hadn't realized how much of a supporter of young people Art really was."

A native of Kansas City, Bobby began his journey to Messengerdom immediately after relocating to the Big Apple in 1976. "I got to New York on August 23—it was my birthday. I started sitting in around town, trying to meet the cats, and I met Curtis Fuller, who took me under his wing. Curtis was playing at a club called Storyville, and he invited me to sit in. The second night I was up there, it was October 11—Art's birthday. Lo and behold Art came to hear me; he sat there listening, and the next thing I know, he's up on stage playing. I heard the sound change, and I look around, and there he is, and he says, 'Blow! Blow!'

"So the set ends, and he grabs me and takes me into the bathroom—the bathroom was the Storyville's 'jazz office'—and asked me what I was doing. I said, 'Nothing. I just got into town.' Then he asks, 'How would you like to join the Jazz Messengers?' I thought about it for half a second, and said, 'Shoot, yeah!' Art says, 'Well, come by my house and get some records. I want you to learn some songs.' So I went up to his apartment on 45th Street, and he comes to the door in his robe and house shoes and gives me a pile of records. I said, 'Thanks, Art,' then *slam*—he shut the door in my face.

"So I went home and got busy. The band was on their way to Japan, but they couldn't get me a visa, so I couldn't go. But Art said that when they got back, they were going to fly me out to San Francisco to the Keystone Korner, and I could start then. In the meantime, I was learning all these songs, and I was going around town telling everybody I was going to join the Messengers. And I would get comments like, *Don't hold your breath, and Art asked me to join in '69, and I'm still waiting to hear from him*—no one really said, *Congratulations.* But I wasn't worried: Art had given me some clothes—he gave me this Sherlock Holmes jacket—and he'd taken me and my wife to dinner.

"But then the band broke up in Japan, so I went home for Christmas. While I was in Kansas City, I got a call from Art's agent, who'd gotten a telegram from Art saying that even though the band had broken up, they were going to try and gig their way back to New York—but there still wouldn't be a ticket for Bobby Watson. I said, 'Ooookay, there it is.' So I decided to stay home for a few months.

"On January 10, I get a call—'Bobby, it's Art. Listen, we're putting together a new band. It's gonna be a sextet. We're rehearsing tomorrow at 3:00. There's a prepaid ticket for you at the airport. I'll see you at 3:00. Put your mother on the phone.' So he talked to my mother for a half an hour, and told her he'd kick my butt if he caught me doing drugs, and that he'd look out for me, and blah blah blah.

"So I go to New York, I get to rehearsal, and all of a sudden, this Russian guy walks in with a trumpet case. Then comes [bassist] Dennis Irwin, and then Walter Davis. We started rehearsing, and a couple of weeks later, we were doing a recording session, and Art asked, 'Does anybody write?' and he looked right at me. So I pulled out [the original compositions] 'Hawkman' and 'Time Will Tell.' I handed them out and bam—an hour later, they were recorded. I'd only been in the band two weeks, and I got two tunes on the record, which made David Schnitter's hair stand up on end."

"Bobby was one of the Messengers' great arrangers and a great, incredible writer," Donald Harrison said. "He was a perfect writer for Art Blakey, in my estimation." Watson's rightness was apparent from the start. Though he'd written "Hawkman" and "Time Will Tell" (*In My Prime 1*) while still in college, both tunes were ready-made for Blakey. The melody of the former is propelled by a swift 6/8 shuffle feel, one of Buhaina's fave grooves, but the solos are in double-time 4/4; with its almost danceable beat and layered harmonies, it comes across as a Benny Golson/Wayne Shorter hybrid. The latter song also has shuffle elements, and while it doesn't have a specific musical antecedent vis-à-vis the Messengers, it's undeniably a Messengers tune—something that bespeaks of Watson's attention to history.

Bobby was a productive writer, but the band waxed only a handful of his tunes; two of the most memorable were "E.T.A." and "In Case You Missed It." Based on the chord changes of John Coltrane's "Lazybird," "E.T.A." was recorded once in 1978 (*In My Prime 1*), then again three years later (*Straight Ahead*, Concord Records), and the difference is striking: Executed at a medium tempo, the earlier rendition allows both the front line and pianist James Williams to glide through their respective two solo choruses. But in 1981, Wynton Marsalis and tenor saxophonist Billy Pierce had replaced Ponomarev and Schnitter, and for whatever reason, the song got sped way the heck up. Not only that, but Watson added a dense unison out-chorus that would have been insanely difficult to play even at the original slower tempo. (Williams, who played on both versions, loved the tune, saying, "You listen to 'E.T.A.,' and you knew Bobby had a special thing going on.")

"In Case You Missed It" (*Album of the Year*) was Bobby's Blakey-era magnum opus, a tune that, in a sense, redefined the Messengers' compositional sound. A non-standard A-A-B-A form, "In Case..." was made up of an evil-sounding vamp and a brightly swinging bridge. Melodically and harmonically, the tune has what can only be described as a contemporary feel, a foreshadowing of the sound that would dominate the post-bop of the 1980s.

(Watson offered up an interesting insight as to how Blakey handled his original compositions, drum-wise: "The first time Art would play a tune, it would be the worst, but then it got better and better and better. By the end of the week, he owned it. That's opposed to people who sight-read—the first time they read it is the best, then it goes downhill from there.")

Improvisationally, Bobby was a ticking time bomb, a full-toned technician who could literally and figuratively blow at any time—a quality that Blakey often felt the need to rein in. "Art would chew us out if we weren't swinging, or if we tried to play the music too cleanly, or if we weren't taking any chances. He'd say, 'I'm not hearing any mistakes up there. Y'all sound like you're playing out of an exercise book.' If we'd get too technical, he'd play stuff at tempos that he knew were hard, and he'd say, 'No doubling up.' We had an arrangement of 'Giant Steps' that we used to do as a shuffle, and he didn't allow any doubling up on it.

"He would also tell me I was circular breathing too much—I'd circular breathe for two or three straight choruses, and he'd say, 'Man, when you do that, the rhythm section has to just *wait* for you.' But I thought I was innovating! I was in New York, making my mark—that was the way I saw it. I was playing birdcalls, all kinds of stuff." Watson mostly heeded Buhaina's desire for relative subtlety, but every once in a while, the time bomb would explode in exhilarating fashion. For his blistering solo on the original samba "Pamela" (*In This Korner*), he shuns any sort of buildup, circular breathing and bird-calling from note one. The audience's enthusiastic applause made it evident that every so often, quietude is completely uncalled-for.

(Donald Harrison could have done with even more Watson pyrotechnics. "Bobby is a phenomenal technician. He can do all that double-tonguing and circular breathing—if you want to get those things together, he's the person you should listen to. I was listening to what Bobby was doing in terms of technique; his technique is incredible. I hadn't developed the double-tonguing to his extent. Bobby Watson is the master of that. He was the person who made me want to develop that. He's something else.")

Had Blakey not thrown him from the Messengers nest, Watson might well have stayed with the band for years to come. "One night when we were playing at Blues Alley in D.C., he told me that he'd invited Branford Marsalis down, and then he said, 'I want you to expand the book to four horns. I want to have two altos.' I said, 'Art, man, that's a lot of work, bro. Why do you want me to do all that writing? Let Branford listen to the stuff and put on his own part—he's a good enough musician.'" But Bobby read the writing on the wall; the beginning of the end was near, a fact that was confirmed only hours later. "After the gig, I rode back in the car with Art, and he said, 'Bobby, we're going to make a change.'"

Though stunned to be on his own, Watson was able to see the huge upside of his situation. "I was tired of the gig, but the security of working a lot was nice. But to work with Art, you have to be young and inexperienced. Once you start learning what's out there, it's time to go. He gives you your start, and when you mature enough to learn the business, and start getting stronger, it's time to move on. But he told me, 'You'll be fine. You can fly. So go ahead and fly.'"

WILLIAM THE CONQUEROR
Billy Pierce

"Billy Pierce is a guy that I'd pay to see."

—Javon Jackson

WHEN A WRITER garners greater respect from his peers than he does from the general public, he's said to be an "author's author."

When a painter confounds critics but receives plaudits from his fellow artists, he's called a "painter's painter."

When an instrumentalist is a cult hero valued by his listeners but revered by his musical brethren, he's dubbed a "musician's musician."

Though the listening public had more than a healthy respect for him, Billy Pierce is the ultimate "musician's musician."

"When I was listening to the Messengers' early-'80s groups," Javon Jackson said, "I looked up to Wynton Marsalis. But all the older musicians would tell me, 'Billy Pierce is playing the most horn in the band.' And they were right. He's a very great, very intellectual saxophonist."

Bobby Watson, who played alongside Pierce for two years, agreed. "Billy's approach to harmony and his technique are at such a high level, I was up in his stuff and listening to him *immediately*. His professionalism, his maturity, and the way he carries himself have always impressed me."

Raised in Florida and educated at Tennessee State University and Berklee College of Music in Boston, Pierce landed his first big-time music gig in 1970, spending eight months as a sideman for Stevie Wonder. After a variety of jobs—including one with Roy Radin's American Vaudeville Review, during which he backed Frank Gorshin, Joanne Worley, some dog acts, and some drunken jugglers—Billy took a teaching post at Berklee in 1975, where he remained until 1979, at which point he answered Buhaina's siren call.

Older and more experienced than your typical incoming Messenger—he was thirty-two when he joined the band in 1980—Pierce was the ideal yang to the yin of his frontline mates Bobby Watson and Wynton Marsalis; where Watson and Marsalis were all energy, all the time, Billy was understatement personified, a musician who could propel a band and entrance an audience while remaining true to his low-key line of attack.

Though their styles bore little in common, Pierce is a spiritual descendant of the very first Jazz Messengers tenorist. Like Hank Mobley, Billy is a steady soloist who, regardless of tempo or dynamic level, always thinks on his feet. Even on a barn burner like Walter Davis's "Gypsy Folk Tales," (*Art Blakey in Sweden*, Evidence, 1981), a tune in which the rhythm section—especially Buhaina—is hammering its brains out, Billy stays grounded, never letting his bandmates dictate his direction. Nonetheless, he could take it to the next level whenever and wherever he wanted: His one chorus on Wayne Shorter's neo-bop classic "Witch Hunt" (*Album of the Year*) is sheer canned heat.

(Just like Shorter, Billy admits that he was somewhat musically shy when he first joined the band; so, just as he did with Shorter, Blakey tried everything within his power to bring Pierce out of his shell. "I know what it takes to make me play," Billy said, "and that's to have somebody back there really driving the vehicle and kicking me in the butt! It was incredible playing with Art. I could see how he changed my concept of playing, and especially my concept of hearing drumming. When I would go back to Boston on breaks to do gigs, it would be really hard to play with anybody else.")

Pierce's finest recorded moment as a Messenger was his performance on the Duke Ellington ballad "In a Sentimental Mood" (*Keystone 3*). With a reverence for Ellington befitting the tune, Billy gives a stylistic shout-out to Ellington's longtime tenorist, Paul Gonsalves, a swinging contrast to the band's ceaseless but timeless hard bopping.

Billy stayed a Messenger until 1983, when he left to sideman with another torrential drummer, Tony Williams. After eight years on and off with Williams, Pierce decided that he didn't want to take the traveling minstrel route, but rather preferred to spend time with his family—and impart his wisdom upon jazz's up-and-comers. Which is why he went back to Berklee, where he took a job as chair of the Woodwind Department.

"He's a studied guy," Jackson said, "and that comes out in his playing. He comes from a lot of different styles, but he always sounds like himself. He puts things together his way. He's made it his life's work to teach other people."

Billy Pierce is a player with a totally original style. Billy Pierce could have had his pick of gigs, but he chose to teach. Billy Pierce's work as a Jazz Messenger is as Jazz Messenger–ish as that of any tenor saxophonist who ever Jazz Messengered.

All of which is why Billy Pierce is the ultimate musician's musician.

I HEARD YOU TWICE THE FIRST TIME
Branford Marsalis

"Branford has great feeling, great technique, and a great alto sound. An impeccable musician."

—Bobby Watson

FOR THE MAJORITY of the second- and third-generation Jazz Messengers, a job with Art Blakey was a dream gig, the jazz version of the Holy Grail.

That wasn't quite the case for one Branford Marsalis.

"My introduction to Art Blakey was the album cover to *Moanin'*," the multi-reedist said. "When [my brother] Wynton and I were younger, we would go through my dad's records, pull 'em out, and look at the covers. We used to make fun of that particular cover, because we thought that Blakey was an exceedingly unattractive man. When Wynton first got the gig with Art Blakey, he called to tell me, and I said, 'Great. Who's Art Blakey?'—you see, I came to jazz late. So Wynton said, 'You know, the drummer.' I said, 'No, I don't know.' Then he said, 'Remember that ugly dude on that album cover with the big face? That's Art Blakey.'"

Fortunately, Branford was an inquisitive sort, and soon grew eager to learn more about "that ugly dude." "I went to a local cheap student record store where you could buy records for five bucks—I was at Berklee College of Music at the time—and I finally bought the record myself. Wynton and I had made fun of the album cover, but it never occurred to us to put it on. But once I put it on, I realized that *Moanin'* is a fantastic record. Boy, isn't that funny? The stupidity of youth"

Soon after Wynton hooked up with Blakey, he dragged his big brother aboard to augment what ultimately became a big band—that is, if you consider a tentet to be a big band. The inexperienced Branford wasn't an official Messenger on his first recorded appearance with the group (*The Jazz Messenger Big Band Live at Montreux and Northsea*, Timeless Records, 1980), but he still managed to acquit himself quite well. On James Williams's speedy blues "Minor Thesis," Marsalis sounds ebullient and bubbly while trading choruses with trombonist Robin Eubanks, coming off as an exemplary hard bopper. (Bobby Watson, who also played on the session, saw

Branford's instinctive connection to the past. "He reminded me a lot of Cannonball Adderley, but he also had a lot of Bird in him.")

Marsalis was fully cognizant of the fact that at that point in his career, he played like everybody but himself—which, from his perspective, wasn't necessarily a bad thing. "I was a little bit more malleable when I first joined the band. That malleability can sometimes be perceived as a weakness, which it wasn't. The hardest thing for a musician to do is to be malleable. First of all, you have to deal with the outside pressure of people expecting you to develop your own sound, like there's a magic pill you can take, or you can just read some book and *do it*. But there's always this expectation that you're going to come up with this sound."

The following year, Branford was hired to join the group on a full-time basis, if only for nepotistic reasons. "I came in through the back door. When Wynton was in the band, he always used to brag about me. So when he temporarily left Blakey's band to go tour with Herbie [Hancock], Art thought that his best way of securing Wynton would be to hire me, even though he didn't really think much of me as a musician at the time. But I think he grew to appreciate my musicianship later."

It's understandable why Blakey later grew to appreciate Marsalis's musicianship, because by the time "later" rolled around, Branford had become a helluva musician. *Keystone 3*—the lone album documenting Branford's official tenure—showcases a burgeoning saxophone stylist, a gentleman who, over the prior two years, had added a pinch of Eric Dolphy and John Coltrane into his Cannonball/Bird concoction, creating a sound well on the road to total originality. His spot on Curtis Fuller's "A La Mode" is more jagged and edgy than his funkier work of the recent past, a lengthy solo that never flags in either energy or ideas.

Branford's non-musical life while with the Messengers, while thick with priceless learning experiences, was often painful and contentious. "Personally, Art and I were just at odds; I don't think he warmed to me until much later. He had a fast lifestyle that he was very proud of, and it was in contrast to my lifestyle. I was more puritanical, and younger, thus a little more self-righteous than I should've been. In retrospect, there were things that went on that I would have handled differently [now], but I could've diffused some of those things with a less self-righteous tone. [For example], one time we were playing in Denmark, and Bu was a little inebriated, and proceeded to curse out the audience. And I walked off the stage. Everybody in the band was like, 'Man, how could you walk off the stage.' But still, I could've just kept my opinions to myself, not made such a big deal out of it. Then again, maybe the circumstances called for that kind of behavior."

Personal self-righteousness notwithstanding, Branford cherished what he learned from Art Blakey during his year as a Messenger. "I had a great musical experience," Branford said. "What changed me musically was that Art taught me how to play the drums. That made me better understand the function of the drums within not only a rhythm section, but also a group context. In my solos, it gave me better options as to things I could play, so I didn't have to rely so much on licks. My solos wound up being less a stream of continuous eighth notes. It allowed me to put a lot more rhythmic variety to my playing."

Marsalis barely touched his alto saxophone after leaving the Jazz Messengers, choosing instead to focus on the tenor and soprano; and in his latter work, his style became distinct to the point that you couldn't hear much Cannonball or Bird left in his playing. But thanks in part to "that ugly dude," you could hear a whole hell of a lot of Branford.

(l to r) Hank Mobley, Horace Silver, and Doug Watkins. Rehearsal for *Hank Mobley and His All Stars* session, 1/13/57.

Photograph by Francis Wolff, courtesy of Mosaic Images.

(l to r) Donald Byrd and Jackie McLean.
Byrd's *Off To The Races* session,
Englewood Cliffs, New Jersey, 12/21/58.

*Photograph by Francis Wolff,
courtesy of Mosaic Images.*

Kenny Dorham. *Una Mas* **session,**
Englewood Cliffs, New Jersey, 4/1/63.

Photograph by Francis Wolff,
courtesy of Mosaic Images.

(l to r) **Lee Morgan and Johnny Griffin. Griffin's *A Blowin' Session*, Hackensack, New Jersey, 4/6/57.**

Photograph by Francis Wolff, courtesy of Mosaic Images.

**Benny Golson.
Art Blakey's *Moanin'*
session, Hackensack,
New Jersey, 10/30/58.**

*Photograph by
Francis Wolff, courtesy
of Mosaic Images.*

**Walter Davis. *Davis Cup*
session, Englewood Cliffs,
New Jersey, 8/2/59.**

*Photograph by Francis Wolff,
courtesy of Mosaic Images.*

Bobby Timmons. Englewood Cliffs, New Jersey, 8/7/60.

Photograph by Francis Wolff, courtesy of Mosaic Images.

***(l to r)* Lee Morgan and Curtis Fuller. Morgan's *City Lights* session, Hackensack, New Jersey, 8/25/57.**

Photograph by Francis Wolff, courtesy of Mosaic Images.

***(l to r)* Lee Morgan, Wayne Shorter, and Art Blakey. Englewood Cliffs, New Jersey, 11/10/59.**

Photograph by Francis Wolff, courtesy of Mosaic Images.

Jymie Merritt. Art Blakey's *Moanin'* session,
Hackensack, New Jersey, 10/30/58.
Photograph by Francis Wolff, courtesy
of Mosaic Images.

(l to r) Freddie Hubbard and Wayne Shorter. Shorter's *Speak No Evil* session, Englewood Cliffs, New Jersey, 12/24/64.

Photograph by Francis Wolff, courtesy of Mosaic Images.

(l to r) Art Blakey and Cedar Walton. Blakey's *Buhaina's Delight* session, Englewood Cliffs, New Jersey, 12/18/61.

Photograph by Francis Wolff, courtesy of Mosaic Images.

Reggie Workman. Lee Morgan's *Infinity* session, Englewood Cliffs, New Jersey, 11/16/65.

Photograph by Francis Wolff, courtesy of Mosaic Images.

Woody Shaw. Horace Silver's *The Jody Grind* session, Englewood Cliffs, New Jersey, 11/23/66.

Photograph by Francis Wolff, courtesy of Mosaic Images.

Valery Ponomarev.
Courtesy of Valery Ponomarev.

**(l to r) Donald Brown, Billy Pierce,
Wynton Marsalis, Charles Fambrough,
Branford Marsalis, and Art Blakey.**

Courtesy of Donald Brown.

Bobby Watson and Art Blakey.

Courtesy of Bobby Watson.

Branford Marsalis.

Photograph by Kwaku Alston.

Terence Blanchard.
Photograph by Carol Friedman.

Robin Eubanks.
Photograph by Ulli Gruber.

Javon Jackson.

Photograph by Michael Wong.

Benny Green.

*Photograph by
Jimmy Katz.*

Geoffrey Keezer.

*Courtesy of
Geoffrey Keezer.*

(l to r) Javon Jackson, Essiet Okun Essiet, Steve
Davis, and Art Blakey. The Iron Horse,
Northampton, Massachusetts, 5/19/90.

Courtesy of Steve Davis.

(l to r) Brian Lynch, Dale Barlow, Steve Davis,
Javon Jackson, Geoff Keezer, Art Blakey, and
Essie Okun Essiet.

Courtesy of Steve Davis.

DUCK SOUP
Donald Harrison

"My main man is Donald Harrison."

—Javon Jackson

"Donald Harrison is my main man."

—Branford Marsalis

"JUST DO IT."

Contemporary pop culture mavens will recognize that phrase as the tag line for a certain ad campaign conducted by a certain sneaker company. But it's also a philosophy that Art Blakey dropped on the main man to many a modern Messengers saxophonist, Donald Harrison.

Harrison was a long way from main-man status when he hooked up with Blakey in 1982, but thanks to the master's guidance, he gained the confidence necessary to musically pursue whatever he felt deserved pursuing. "Art always encouraged me to work at what I thought was important," said the altoist (and periodic sopranist) known to his friends as "Duck." "I was trying to put the whole history of music into my style. I was [trying to play] everything from traditional New Orleans style all the way to the avant-garde. I was trying to come up with something that dealt with all of that. I used to have arguments with Wynton [Marsalis]—who didn't like New Orleans music [at the time]—and he'd say, 'What're you doing?' Of course Art Blakey would say, 'Just do it.'"

Bobby Watson felt that Harrison succeeded in drawing together those many disparate musical elements. "Donald has a natural swing, but he also has a lot of funk in his playing. His sound is really dark, just the kind of alto sound I like. He carries everything with him at all times."

Javon Jackson also admired Harrison's stylistic range. "He likes to play all kinds of different melodies and bop-type phrases. For my generation of saxophone players, he is at the top of the list."

Like his frontline partner Terence Blanchard, Harrison wasn't far from infancy when he initially encountered Buhaina. "I first met Art through Billy Pierce when I was nineteen years old. I was Billy Pierce's student at Berklee, and when Art came to town, [Pierce] told Art that I was really talented, and he introduced us. When I met him, I didn't have my saxophone with me, and Art looked at me and said, 'Well, where's your horn? Get it and come and play.' I was like, 'No, no, I don't want to do that,' but he insisted that I get my horn and play. So I went back to school and got my horn. And that one time sitting in with Art Blakey changed my playing, because I felt another level of energy and maturity from the rest of the players, which showed me what I had to do to be on that level. It was surreal. It felt like a dream." (It should be noted that Branford Marsalis believed it was he and not Billy Pierce who "discovered" Harrison. "He's a great saxophone player," Marsalis said, "and I recommended him for the gig.")

Harrison absorbed Buhaina's lessons as well as anybody who ever crossed the Messengers threshold, if only because he's an acute observer of human nature—just like Blakey himself. "I'm a guy that watches and listens. I just find that if you talk too much and always have something to say, there's nothing you can learn. When I joined the Messengers, everybody in the band thought they knew everything—there was a lot of back and forth, trying to prove to each other that our way was the right way. Which, in turn, gives you a lot of new ideas. And Art would never say anything while we were going back and forth, and I eventually realized why: He wanted us to share our ideas."

Donald noted that Blakey wasn't merely a hard bopper, but also a self-made world musicologist. "Art would say, 'If you're playing the blues, play the blues. If you're playing Latin music, play Latin music.' I remember we were playing a Latin tune with the band, and he gave us percussion instruments, and he knew all the rhythms necessary for each instrument. When I played with [Latin pianist/composer] Eddie Palmieri and really studied that kind of music, I realized that Art really knew what he was doing. A lot of the younger jazz musicians play random rhythms that sort of sound like it might be Latin, but it's not really. You listen to somebody like [drummer] Roy Haynes, or Elvin Jones, or Art Blakey, and they *know*—trust me. When I really started studying the specifics of different musics, I realized that the older musicians really knew exactly what was going on in every style. It made me want to really know things, and not just skirt over them."

Also like Blanchard, Harrison's musical growth during his four years with the band was astounding. His work on the title cut of his 1982 Messengers debut *Oh, By the Way* (Timeless Records) is frenetic and choppy, irrefutably exhilarating but dynamically limited. Fast-forward to the 1985 live session *Hard Champion* (ProJazz Records) and his improv on "Witch Hunt."

He kicks off this solo with some quiet, chromatic-based eighth notes, which lead into a series of staccato octave leaps, which lead into a series of repetitive atonal motifs, which lead into a series of warp-speed double- and triple-time runs; he builds from beginning to end, the ideas and vivacity never waning. It was Blakey's encouragement that encouraged Harrison to elevate himself. "Art would always tell me, 'Hey, when you're working on some new stuff, I want to help you in any kind of way. Whatever you're thinking about, just tell me.'"

But Donald—like most every Messenger—knew that being in the band wasn't all about playing. "You *had* to write," Harrison said. "You had to continue to grow." And while Donald didn't compose a huge number of tunes for the group, his songs were uniformly solid, and again, like his playing, his growth was astounding. Heard on *Oh, By the Way*, his first recorded composition, "Duck Soup," is a straight-up bopper—not even a hard bopper, but an old-timey bebopper—based on the chord changes of Charlie Parker's standard "Confirmation." "Duck Soup" was a pleasant tune, but it's not nearly as fresh as "Mr. Combinated." (*Blue Night*, Timeless Records, 1985) A muscular post-bop tome, the thirty-two-bar jam differs from his first composition thanks to the non-standard form, the quirkily chromatic chord changes, and the dark, almost sinister vibe.

From Harrison's perspective, the modern Messengers saxophone lineage—from Bobby Watson on—was in and of itself as rich and vital as the Mobley-to-Golson-to-Shorter period. "I don't think a lot of young musicians want to acknowledge that we really listened to each other. But Branford listened to me, and I listened to [future Messengers altoist] Kenny [Garrett], and he listened to Bobby Watson. All of us listened to each other. We all sounded like ourselves, but we were all influenced by each other." But Branford believed that Duck was one of the most important links in the chain, if not *the* most important. "The Donald Harrison era was really fertile and creative, for my ears," Branford said.

Like all of Blakey's most fervent disciples, Harrison utilized many of Buhaina's lessons throughout his post-Messengers life, but one message stood out above the rest: "The most important thing Art Blakey always used to say was, 'If you're doing something right, at some point, people are going to acknowledge it. So just keep doing what you do.'" And as usual, Buhaina was right: People definitely acknowledged that Donald Harrison was doing something—because Donald Harrison *just did it.*

A JACKSON IN THE HOUSE
Javon Jackson

"Javon Jackson's got 'Messenger' written all over him."
—Bobby Watson

WAS ART BLAKEY the best man at Benny Golson's wedding? Nope.

Was Art Blakey the best man at Wayne Shorter's wedding? Nope.

Was Art Blakey the best man at Javon Jackson's wedding? Yup.

That demonstrates Javon Jackson's unconditional, unadulterated love for Abdullah Ibn Buhaina, and also demonstrates Art Blakey's unconditional, unadulterated love for his final tenor saxophonist.

"Being with the Messengers helped Javon blossom into a monster musician," Bobby Watson said; he felt that Jackson's road to monsterdom stemmed in part from that reciprocal affection. "He hung out with Art about as much as I did. Art really, really loved Javon. And Javon really got to know and love Art."

In a sense, Javon was predestined to adore Blakey. "It was a dream for me to play with the Jazz Messengers ever since I was thirteen or fourteen," Jackson said. "My father was a big jazz listener, so I'd heard all the records. That was my motivation at the start." It wasn't long before the Missouri-born, Denver-raised Jackson made inroads to realizing his goal. "When I was sixteen, I was in the McDonald's All-American High School Band. [Trombonist] Delfeayo Marsalis was in the band with me, and it was through him that I met Branford Marsalis. At that point, Wynton and Branford had just come on the scene, and began to make some noise. Branford was someone I was interested in, and I told him [about] my desire to be in the Messengers band. He said, 'You should go to Berklee first, and study with Billy Pierce.' So I went to Berklee, and I studied with Pierce and [former Messengers pianist] Donald Brown. Donald was very instrumental in helping me out. After [tenor saxophonist] Jean Toussaint left the group, there was an opening, so I went and sat in at Mikell's. Donald had taught me a couple of the songs, but when I sat in, we didn't play any of those songs. I played a tune with 'I Got Rhythm' chord changes, and Art said, 'If you can, I'd like you to come back tomorrow night.' So I did, and after that, he asked me to join the group. I was on cloud nine."

The then-twenty-one-year-old's introduction to the jazz world was fast and furious. "When I joined the group in 1987, I'd been at Berklee for two years; within the first two weeks of playing with Art Blakey, everything I'd learned there was wiped out. He told me immediately, 'You've gotta get your sound together—I can't hear you.' Plus, when you're in the Jazz Messengers, you're on the road, you're traveling, you're out there playing with the cats, the guys that come and sit in with you, guys like Benny Golson, or Jackie McLean, or Wayne Shorter, or Freddie Hubbard. Plus, Max Roach would come to the gig, or Roy Haynes, or [activist] Julian Bond, or [comedian] Bill Cosby, or whoever. To see those guys, and to see their interest in you because of the fact you're with Art Blakey, that was extremely wonderful."

But the lessons weren't just musical. "I was just a college kid. I felt like I grew up into a man with Art Blakey. It was the responsibilities: I was on the road, I was living in New York on my own, I had to pay my own rent, I had to pay bills, I had to be responsible for my laundry, I had to maintain my money. In college, I didn't have to deal with any of that. My mom would send me forty or fifty bucks, and every Christmas I'd go home. I was weaning myself, but I wasn't out there on my own. Also, everybody wants the [Messengers] gig, so you always watch your p's and q's. You don't know whether you're going to last or not. You have that insecurity to battle with, too."

Though young, inexperienced, and admittedly insecure, Jackson carved a niche for himself almost immediately. "My strong point was that I could swing. I had good feeling and a good sound." All of those attributes are on display throughout Javon's first Messengers studio recording, *Not Yet* (Soul Note, 1987). Rhythmically, his eighth notes on "Falling in Love With Love" are swung hard in a traditional-style swing-cum-early-bop fashion, but his progressive harmonies place him firmly in the hard bop camp.

As was the case with every young, impressionable Messenger, Javon's overall musicianship improved with each passing month in the band. By the time 1990 rolled around, Jackson's playing, writing, and arranging skills were in full flower. The loping stop-start "Kay Pea" (*Chippin' In*) could have come from the pen of Hank Mobley; as most modern Messengers composers looked to Wayne Shorter or Cedar Walton for inspiration, Jackson's tune is a rarity. In contrast, "Theme for Penny"—his lone original on *One for All*—demonstrates Javon's flexibility, utilizing the eternally state-of-the-art chord structure of John Coltrane's "Giant Steps."

"Javon was really *there* for Art on another level, both on and off the bandstand," Bobby Watson said—and that meant through sickness and health. Over those final few years of his life, Art Blakey began to lose his hearing, and though that piece of information was common knowledge in the jazz world, Javon—even though he helped take care of Art in every way he could—believed that Buhaina might have been fudging the seriousness of his ailment. "In my opinion, his deafness was a little exaggerated, and it was exaggerated by him. He didn't hear well out of one ear, but he heard fine out of the other one. He could hear you when played something badly, and he was quick to say, 'Hey, you missed that there.' But anything like, 'I might not be available for the next gig,' all of a sudden it was like, 'Huh? I can't hear you.'" (Jackson's Messenger-mate Geoffrey Keezer was also suspicious of Art's disorder. "He was selectively deaf. He would go deaf when you'd ask him about money, but if things were quiet and you sat and talked to him one-on-one, he'd hear you just fine.")

The Blakey/Jackson love affair was a multitiered one. There was a whole heap of heartfelt, father-and-son-like affection, but the relationship really stemmed from a mutual sense of musical respect. "Art Blakey has the highest level of individuality," Jackson said. "His style was so personal. You can't sound like Art Blakey."

And the saxophonist learned that lesson well, because *his* style is so personal. In other words, you can't sound like Javon Jackson.

SAXOPHONE NOTES

JOHNNY GRIFFIN was one of the few musicians who came into the Jazz Messengers armed with the in-yo'-face demeanor needed to hang musically with Art Blakey. "Johnny Griffin, you're talking about fire," Javon Jackson said. "You're talking about headiness. You're talking about a giant. In any key, at any tempo, in any type of song, he was what you'd call a real master of the tenor saxophone. Fire and brimstone, man. He plays fast, he plays all night."

Even though Griff was a jazz veteran when he joined the group in 1957, his year-plus with Blakey was still more than just another gig. "My experience in Art's band was excellent because that's exactly the style of music I like to play—very explosive, strong, fire all the time. We used to have games, like warfare, between the front line and back line—the horns and the rhythm section. There was a spirit of competition, but in a playful and positive spirit."

A seeming stylistic mismatch, tenorist **John Gilmore**'s tenure with the Jazz Messengers was brief but explosive—and, sadly, virtually undocumented on wax. Best known for his long-term association with pianist/composer/innovator/dude-from-outer-space Sun Ra, Gilmore was a volatile improviser, given to utilizing atonal honks and squeals to get his point across.

In his six months with the Messengers beginning in 1964, the tenorist's frontline mate was fonkay fonkay Lee Morgan, a player whose bluesiness stood in sharp but awe-inspiring contrast to Gilmore's thinking-out-of-the-box-ed-ness. If nothing else, having him in the band proved that Art Blakey was one open-minded bandleader.

"The next great [Jazz Messengers altoist] after Jackie McLean would be **Gary Bartz**," Donald Harrison said. "You can really hear Jackie's influence in his playing."

If you do a side-by-side, Pepsi Challenge kind of thing with records featuring Harrison and Gary Bartz, you'll glean that Duck isn't merely paying lip service when he said, "For my money, Gary is one of the heavyweights on the alto saxophone who people are not really dealing with. He continues to be an influence."

"That band with **Jean Toussaint**, Donald Harrison, and Terence Blanchard was great and under-recognized," said Branford Marsalis. And while Harrison and Blanchard were the heralded members of that particular ensemble, tenorist Toussaint was a big part of what made that band tick.

Born on St. Thomas in the Virgin Islands, Jean was a poster boy for modern Messenger saxophone acumen. A spiritual brother of Billy Pierce, Toussaint was the archetypal Blakey tenorman, a thoughtful, unselfish—if underappreciated—soloist who graced the band between 1982 and 1986.

Along with Jackie McLean, Wayne Shorter, Gary Bartz, Keith Jarrett, and Branford Marsalis, **Kenny Garrett** is one of the few musicians who spent significant chunks of time sidemanning with both Art Blakey and Miles Davis.

Bobby Watson loved Garrett's energy ("Kenny plays with a lot of intensity. I just dig him"), but is mildly envious of Kenny's career direction ("I wish I'd gotten the gig with Miles").

It's understandable why both Blakey and Davis were enraptured by Garrett's sax work, as he straddles the line beautifully between old-school hard bop and new-school funk. "I hear a lot of pop influences in what Kenny Garrett was doing, plus some Cannonball," Donald Harrison said. Javon Jackson recognized this all-encompassing quality, noting, "The first guys Kenny heard were Hank Crawford and Grover Washington, Jr. But harmonically, he's coming from Coltrane."

Garrett took full advantage of his time with Blakey. "That was an institution, playing with Blakey. He taught me how to play in a short amount of time because there were so many other horn players there and everybody needed a chance to express themselves. You'd get like two choruses, maybe three choruses, and then you'd have to get out of there. He would give you a press roll, which indicated that it was time to play. The first chorus, you can mess around, then he'd give you that press roll and then it was time to play. It was a great experience. I learned a lot, some things about being a bandleader, what to do and some things not to do. That was a stepping-stone."

Finally, from the Department of What-Could-Have-Been:

In a 1976 interview, Art Blakey said, "[After Benny Golson left the band], it was a toss-up between John Coltrane and Wayne Shorter [to replace him]. But John Coltrane had been working with Thelonious Monk, and I didn't want to take him away."

Talk about altering the course of jazz history…

THE PIANISTS
Roots and Herbs

"Art Blakey loved the piano. He was a piano freak."

—Benny Green

BENNY GREEN was right—Art Blakey was a piano freak. But some of the Jazz Messengers might not automatically agree with that: Freddie Hubbard might claim that Bu was a trumpet freak, while Javon Jackson probably believed the drummer was a saxophone freak. Still, Green's assertion that the piano was the number one instrument on Buhaina's freak parade is most likely legit, if only because Blakey began his musical life as a keyboardist. And then there's the fact that while the horn players were the most visible Messenger superstars, it was often the pianists who anchored, if not held together, the band.

James Williams contended that it was vital that the gentleman (or lady) who sat on the piano bench bring more to the table than just hot licks. "It was important that the person in the piano chair be an arranger, because Art depended on us having music. Because each edition of the band should have had its own sound within the context of the Jazz Messengers."

Apparently it was also a prerequisite for the piano player to be a kind, honorable individual. "All the pianists happened to be positive people," Horace Silver said. "The Messenger pianists I knew were all nice cats, and none were egotistical or braggadocious. They were all down to earth. They were just nice people." (Joanne Brackeen observed that it wasn't difficult for Buhaina to track down cool keyboardists: "I don't know many piano players that *aren't* nice people. Maybe that's just a trait of piano players.")

Aside from niceness, the ivory ticklers had something else in common: They always made it a point to check each other out. Like most of the second- and third-generation Messenger pianists, Geoffrey Keezer was digging the boys in the band early on in his musical development. "When I was younger, I went through a period where I transcribed all the Messenger pianists' solos."

In terms of the lineage, Green—who, like Keezer, was an adolescent Messenger-phile—felt that his predecessors made it easy for a young buck such as himself to step right in, make some noise, and preserve the pianistic tradition. "If you took Horace Silver, Bobby Timmons, and Cedar Walton out of the picture, I couldn't imagine what playing with Art would be. They pretty much defined how it sounds and how it feels to be at one with Art."

YEAH!
Horace Silver

"One of the main ingredients of the Jazz Messengers was the soulful, bluesy, gospel sound of Horace Silver. He helped shape the sound of the band for generations."

—Mulgrew Miller

HORACE SILVER is a modest chap, but this modesty doesn't blind him to the reality that he had an enormous impact on both jazz and the Jazz Messengers. Another reality is that Horace—aside from maybe Wayne Shorter—was the most historically significant of all the Messengers sidemen. The perceptive Silver was well aware of his bearing on the band: "I'm not trying to be egotistical, but I would say that most of the [future Messenger] pianists drew from my playing. They probably felt an influence from me. I'm not saying that they copied me, but there was a slight influence there."

It's more than an understatement to say that Horace had only a slight influence on the post-Silver Jazz Messenger writers, because, as pianist Mulgrew Miller explained, "One of the things that helped mold the sound of the band other than Art's drumming was the compositional talents of Horace Silver." Geoffrey Keezer put it even more succinctly: "Horace Silver, through his compositions, basically defined the Jazz Messengers style."

Blakey, in part, was responsible for prodding Silver into becoming a complete musician. "[Horace] was very shy when he came in," Buhaina said, "and I told him, besides playing you've got to write. So he started writing, and his writing was good. He kept it up and he was going—his music [was] beautiful. He learned how to voice very well. He learned how to utilize two horns to the fullest extent. That's one thing I learned from him—instead of hearing a whole lot of horns, he'd take two horns and get just as much out of two as you can get out of three in most cases. He would utilize everything. He just turned out to be a hell of an arranger. The more he did it, the better he got."

Horace took to small-band writing the way Duke Ellington took to big-band writing. "Art was not a composer," Silver said, "so he relied on the guys in the band to provide the material. It was a great venue for me to experiment with my writing." In terms of form and chordal structure, his songs were indeed experimental—but part of what made them so special is that his tuneful tunes didn't *sound* experimental, but rather swinging and accessible. "Nica's Dream," Horace's most celebrated Messengers composition, is a mid-tempo Latino-bopper, similar to Benny Golson's "Whisper Not" in the sense that it's at once harmonically intricate and melodically affable. And while his songs were complex, musicians still ate them up; the band's rendition of "Nica" times out at a lengthy eleven-plus minutes; it was almost as if the soloists couldn't stop tap dancing over the changes. And "Stop Time" (*Horace Silver and the Jazz Messengers*) is a sixteen-bar jam whose chord changes don't resolve in a traditional II-V-I manner, giving it an unusual sense of perpetual motion that lights a fire under the soloists.

The impact of Horace's pen on eventual Messenger authors was intense and indisputable. "Probably after Bird, I knew more Horace Silver compositions than any other composer," Donald Brown said. "Even before I joined the Messengers, compositionally, he was probably—along with Monk and Bird and Miles—the one individual composer that I really *listened* to. It was the band sound, how the horns were orchestrated around the piano. I really learned a lot about composing and arranging just by studying Horace."

In a display of modesty, Horace downplayed the effect his pianisms had in sculpting the Messenger sonority, viewing his work as just another part of his musical growth. "Being in the band molded my playing because it gave me a chance to experiment. Playing with a group steadily, playing every night, was a great opportunity."

The steady work no doubt improved his chops, but Silver, as Joanne Brackeen noted, came into the band with a style that was all but fully formed. "Horace Silver was amazing," Joanne Brackeen said. "When he came up, the cats were Thelonious Monk, Bud Powell, and Horace—and everybody sounded different. And Horace just kept playing the way he played."

Benny Green felt Silver was not only a formidable soloist, but also a brilliant accompanist. "At the time that Horace came on the scene, all the young pianists were trying their best to play like Bud Powell—not that they could, but Bud was the prevalent influence at the time. But Horace was the first guy to come along since Bud's appearance to have his own approach to comping. He was certainly influenced by Bud, and Monk, and others, but he had his own personality, which you can hear from his very first recordings. In that sense, Horace was a real trailblazer. That's a really heavy thing—to play with true individuality when everybody is doing it one specific way. That's true artistry."

"Horace's style was very interesting," Cedar Walton said. "It was a combination of his playing, and his compositions, and his bandmates—I find it difficult to separate the composite of Horace, Kenny Dorham, and Hank Mobley—that helped make that group impeccable. When I heard Art's desire to combine funk with sophistication, it made a lot of sense to me. Horace fit right in."

To be sure, his playing throughout *Horace Silver and the Jazz Messengers* is indeed funky and sophisticated, an exemplary model of the vibe that would dominate jazz in the mid-to-late 1950s. On "To Whom It May Concern"—another fresh-sounding Silver original—Horace's left-hand work is the picture of post-bop minimalism, a combination of single bass notes and sporadic three-finger chords, all of which transmuted his right-handed Monk-and-Powell-isms into straight-up Silver.

Brown felt that Silver's keyboard efforts were enhanced by his simpatico-ness with Blakey. "What Horace brought to the band was that funkiness. He stretched the groove. When you think about those records with Horace, you think about the fact that the band swings *intensely*. And Horace anchored down the rhythm section, along with Art. When it comes to rhythm sections, you usually talk about piano/bass hookups, but definitely with Bu, it was a serious piano/drum hookup."

Blakey was well aware of the synergy between himself and his pianist. "I had a ball playing with [Horace] in the rhythm section. We seemed to fit together. When he got his own groups he wanted all his drummers to play in the same style as I was trying to play. We always got along musically as well as spiritually and otherwise." Their closeness was evident both on and off the bandstand. "[Horace] was very quiet and very nice to me," Blakey continued. "One night on TV—I don't know where he was—he said, 'I really thank God for Art Blakey because he really got on me and helped me to go on and start writing.' And that made me feel so good. I've never forgotten it. And we've been tight ever since. We've been very good friends."

Even in the band's infancy, Blakey was already in teacher mode, and despite the fact that he was at first the band's ostensible leader, Silver was a more than willing student. "Art was a great guy and one hell of a drummer.

One great thing that I think I learned from Art is to give all of yourself when you get up on that bandstand. That bandstand is like an altar—it's like holy ground or sacred ground. When you get up on that stage or that bandstand, throw everything else out of your mind and just give one hundred percent or one hundred and fifty percent of yourself. Give your all. I remember one time, Art was giving us a lecture at the Café Bohemia. I guess he wasn't satisfied as to what the band was doing. He said, 'Look, you guys. I don't care if you had a fight with your girlfriend or with your wife, or whatever problems you have got outside. When you come into this club, leave that shit outside and come up here onto this bandstand and let's take care of business. When you want to pick them problems up when you go home, that's your business. When you come in here, leave that shit outside and let's get up on there and cook.' Get up on the bandstand and take care of business—and that's what he did. That's what he encouraged us all to do."

Buhaina's encouragement worked. Horace Silver always left his shit outside. Horace Silver always got on up there and cooked.

Horace Silver *always* took care of business.

SOULFUL MR. TIMMONS
Bobby Timmons

"Bobby Timmons is one of those guys you hear when you're a kid, and think, 'Man, I wish I could be this person.'"

—Donald Brown

WITH HIS SYNCOPATED, sophisticated rhythmic approach and aggressively sweaty attitude, James Brown was one of contemporary pop music's original funksters. Brown's disciple George Clinton modernized this newfangled funk conception, modifying J.B.'s grooves with an eye on both the past and the present.

With his Bud-Powell-goes-to-church pianistic approach and aggressively sweaty attitude, Horace Silver was one of contemporary hard bop's original funksters. Silver's disciple Bobby Timmons modernized this newfangled funk conception, modifying Horace's grooves with an eye on both the past and the present.

"Like Horace, Bobby Timmons had that bluesy, soulful sound that helped further the history of the Jazz Messengers," Mulgrew Miller said.

Yet another one of those ubiquitous Philly-born Messenger phenomena, Bobby—who joined the band in 1958—recognized that he was loaded with soul, but wasn't able to pinpoint its source. "Soul is an innate thing in people," Timmons said. "Some people do have it, and some don't. You can't just snatch it and throw it around like it's nothing. You can't just decide to be soulful. If you have soul, it will be there. And if the person listening has soul, he'll recognize it." (Cedar Walton had a plausible theory as to how Timmons attained his high level of soulfulness: "Timmons's father was a minister in Philadelphia, so he had that gospel background. Bobby wrote a lot of successful songs with the Messengers in that [gospel] vein, which, for him, kind of was a priority.")

Benny Green noted that Timmons's harmonic and rhythmic spirituality was apparent to both listeners and peers alike. "Jimmy Heath once told me, 'Pretty much any song that Bobby Timmons played, he'd take it to church. *Anything.*' His sound blended so beautifully with Art's drumming that I definitely spent a lot of my time with the Messengers really trying to assimilate what Bobby Timmons did, in my own fashion."

It might have seemed that Timmons wouldn't have much of a chance to attend that hypothetical musical house of worship, especially considering that during the latter part of his two-year-plus Messengers tenure, Wayne Shorter was the band's primary composer, and the saxophonist was, in a sense, a compositional agnostic. Wayne's blazing "The Summit" (*Meet You at the Jazz Corner of the World*, Blue Note, 1960) is a typical Shorter tune, if there is such a thing, up-tempo with a distinctly un-funky set of chord changes, but Timmons nonetheless sprinkles a whole heap of groovy blues notes and greasy trills throughout, momentarily turning Wayne's hard bop labyrinth into a bully pulpit for testifyin'. "Noise in the Attic" (*Like Someone in Love*, Blue Note, 1960) is another Shorter gem, a speed demon with a set of modal chord changes that are virtually impossible to layer with funk—but somehow Timmons manages by skating into a Horace Silver-esque minimalist mode, liberally loading his improv with well-placed minor thirds and an assortment of bouncy rhythmic motifs.

Shorter, as noted, was outrageously prolific, thus it was often tough for his bandmates to wedge their tunes into the Messengers songbook—but Bobby was able to slip a few gems into the repertoire, all of which bore his funky thumbprints. "Bobby wrote some hits for the band," Miller said, "and helped establish the Messengers as a popular unit, partly because he was both soulful and well rooted in that early bebop thing."

"Moanin'" was, of course, Timmons's biggest "hit," another one of those sounds-easy-but-really-isn't tunes so endemic to Blakey's troupe. "You'd hear 'Moanin'' and think, 'Anybody can play this stuff,'" James Williams said, "but wasn't easy to capture the right feel, to capture what Bobby had in mind. We had to play those songs every night as if it was the first time we were playing them; we had to sound fresh and play creative ideas without overstating or overplaying the piece. We'd have to play *the song*, instead of getting out all of our slick little ideas. It took a while for us to learn that—but we *did* learn it."

Other than the *über*-churchy "Dat Dere," (*The Big Beat*), none of Bobby's other originals captured the jazz world's imagination, which is unfortunate, considering that "So Tired" (*A Night in Tunisia*) and "A Little Busy" (*The Witch Doctor*) are as interesting as the so-called hits, if not more so. The former is an even-eighth-noted boogaloo that predated Lee Morgan's similarly grooved smash "The Sidewinder" by almost three years. And the latter is Bobby's most fully realized Messengers-era tune, a taut finger-snapper incorporating Lee Morgan's energy, Thelonious Monk's humor, and Wayne Shorter's freshness.

Timmons didn't have the widespread influence of a Horace Silver or a Benny Golson, but his multifaceted conception touched those musicians in the know. "He's one of the players I wish I could play like," Donald Brown said. "He wasn't a flashy player, but everything was in the right place, he swung, and every solo had a story behind it. He was the ultimate sideman, but when it was time for him to shine as a leader, he had his own sound with his trio—that big, warm sound. I loved to hear him play ballads, and I loved to hear him play something funky. His playing was beautiful, no matter how simple or complex it was."

Horace Silver believed Timmons to be an exceptionally kind, charismatic individual, and felt that his demeanor had a direct effect on his music. "Bobby was a beautiful person, always telling you jokes, making you laugh. He had a very humorous personality, and that definitely translated into his playing."

Even though he went on to produce an enduring body of work, Bobby Timmons contended that his time with the Jazz Messengers was the high point of his career. Come 1961, Timmons knew it was time to leave the Jazz Messengers nest, and while he was ready to embark on a solo career, he knew that he was walking away from something magical. "There is really no other group to go to from here—I couldn't find anything in any other group that I can't find [here]. The most important thing with the Messengers is that you never have to worry about that swing. As long as Art's there, that [swing is] always there."

SCORPIO RISING
Walter Davis Jr.

> "*Walter Davis was a beautiful cat. And he sure could play his ass off.*"
>
> —Horace Silver

A BRIEF ANECDOTE, courtesy of Benny Green:

"At Walter Davis's funeral, Art Blakey walked up to the podium and said, 'I see none of y'all learned a damn thing from Walter. Your lower lips are all hanging down so low that if you stood up, you'd trip over 'em. Walter Davis was a happy man. He lived with an enjoyment of life, and if you learn anything from him, it should be that.'"

That joie de vivre was both felt and heard in every note played and every song written by Walter Davis Jr.

Davis's musical ebullience stemmed in part from his reverence of bebop history. "Walter Davis was one of the heaviest practitioners of the Bud Powell school," Cedar Walton said. "He used to hang out with Bud, and would describe to me how Bud impressed him when he was in his prime. I was glad that I knew somebody who had a firsthand impression and experience with seeing Bud."

"Walter is probably the person who most authentically captured the flavor of Bud Powell," James Williams said, "and not just playing the notes and the phrases. He had all the subtleties and nuances of Bud's playing, as well as the explosiveness." (Davis's love for Powell was equaled only by Powell's love for Davis, as demonstrated by Bud's trust in Walter's interpretive abilities. "Bud used to teach Walter his compositions," Williams said, "and then Bud would listen to him play [the tunes] so he could listen to them played.")

Mulgrew Miller endorsed Williams's verdict. "While Walter really brought that Bud Powell thing to the band—which he was so widely known for—he didn't make as much impact on the overall sound of the group as Bobby Timmons or Horace Silver, but he was certainly a significant player."

While he didn't specifically modify the group's paradigm, Davis had a heavy impact on a considerable number of Messengers keyboardsmen, most notably Mr. Williams himself. "I didn't appreciate Walter as much when I first heard him, because I was into other pianists like Herbie Hancock, McCoy

Tyner, Chick Corea, Phineas Newborn, and Oscar Peterson. I dug Bud, but I wasn't hearing Walter Davis; he didn't captivate me at that time. But the rapport when he would play with Art—they had a special intuitive thing together, and I picked up on that *very* quickly. I tried to emulate that, so in a sense, if I had to say any one pianist influenced me more than any of the Jazz Messengers—even Horace or Bobby—it probably would be Walter Davis. He gave me an idea of how I was supposed to function as an accompanist in the Jazz Messengers. I needed to be able to convince Art that I could do that, so I could earn his trust."

Donald Brown was also touched by Davis's approach. "There was something especially original about Walter Davis Jr. [He had] another sound. He was one of the players that people slept on; he might have been overlooked as a Messenger. He was an *incredible* pianist, and he really pushed the envelope and stretched the harmonies."

Yes, Davis's note and chord choices were generally one step ahead, but it was all done in such a melodic, comprehensible fashion that even his bandmates might not have realized how flat-out hip he sounded. His confident navigation through Wayne Shorter's gorgeous up-tempo waltz "United" (*Roots and Herbs*, Blue Note, 1961) is striking if only because he was able to translate Shorter's Byzantine chord changes into English. And his single-note-rooted, hornlike spot on his original composition "Splendid" (*Africaine*) is simply masterful.

A distinctly quirky tune, "Splendid" was an antecedent to Walter's mature writing style. "Walter brought a *heavy* compositional thing to the band," Miller said.

"Art really loved Walter's writing," Williams said. "We didn't keep that many Wayne Shorter tunes in the book, and other than 'Moanin',' we didn't play any other Bobby Timmons tunes. But the tunes that survived—from all the editions that I was in, right down to the bands with Benny Green and Geoffrey Keezer—were some of the Walter D. tunes."

"Jody," "Uranus," and "Gypsy Folk Tales" are unquestionably Davis's most venerated, most durable compositions, all of which, as Williams remarked, were in the Messengers book until the end. While each is inventive unto itself, all three share traits indigenous to Walter's later period writing: All feature slick piano/bass unison lines and tension-building pedal points; all are modal-based; all are warp-speed fast; and all are astonishingly difficult to execute. At the risk of slighting some fine ensembles, there's only one Davis tune waxed by the Messengers—"Jody" on *In My Prime Volume 1*—that could be considered just right.

Walter Davis Jr. never reached the heights of Silver or Timmons, but James Williams contended that in Blakey's mind, the Buhaina/Davis hookup was as good as it got. "Art had a special thing with Walter. If he wasn't Art's favorite pianist, he was *very* close."

FIRM ROOTS
Cedar Walton

"Cedar Walton's approach to the band was consummate. He exemplified what it was to be a Messenger."

—Steve Davis

JAMES WILLIAMS knows and respects the Jazz Messengers lineage as well as any pianist who preceded or followed him. "The four people who really established the piano sound for the Messengers—and defined it right on down to the end—would be Horace Silver, Bobby Timmons, Walter Davis, and Cedar Walton," Williams said. "The rest of us are just imitators of what they were doing. They set the tone for what the piano chair should sound like. But Cedar came in behind Walter, and that was a really difficult thing; it was a challenge."

The Dallas-born Walton not only met that challenge, but also established an up-to-the-minute Jazz Messengers rhythm section groove, a sound personified by impeccable note placement, modernized harmonic complexity, on-point comping, and a laid-back sense of swing-bop—all of which both complemented and enhanced Art Blakey's percussion.

"Cedar has always been one of the most criminally underrated pianists in the world," Mulgrew Miller said. "He's a terrific musician, and is gifted in many areas: One, as a melodic improviser, he has few peers; two, out of all the Messenger piano players, he was the best orchestrator. He had the most orchestral approach, which has made him the best post-Messenger trio player."

"Cedar is one of my top ten favorite pianists," Donald Brown said. "He was the guy that, when I joined the band, I related to musically more than anybody. He brought another level of sophistication to the band. He's one of our greatest composers not just today, but in the history of the music. He was the perfect pianist to go with that Freddie Hubbard/Wayne Shorter/Curtis Fuller band. He had the total package—he played the hell out of the ballads, he sounded great comping behind soloists, his arrangements were great, and his introductions to tunes were great. The records he was on, I was just mesmerized by them."

Though only twenty-seven when he joined the Messengers in 1961, Walton was a hard bop veteran of sorts. "Cedar was a major influence in the band," Williams said, "partly because he'd been around for a little bit, recording and playing with Lou Donaldson and Clifford Jordan, making some records on his own."

His hands-on experience helped make the transition from freelance sideman to Messengers sideman that much more fulfilling. "Freddie Hubbard and I joined the band the same day that Lee Morgan and Bobby Timmons were vacating their positions," Walton said. "I was in Chicago with the [Benny Golson/Art Farmer] Jazztet, and Art called me and said, 'Okay, Cedar, come on.' I'd met him years before, which was a good thing, because it gave me the opportunity [to play with the band], and I seized it. I brought [the original composition] 'Mosaic' to my first rehearsal, and next thing I knew, we'd recorded it, and it was the name of the album. That was a good time for me."

Williams believed that it took Walton a while to find his niche, but once he got his footing, it was look out below. "The band Cedar was in was so dynamic, he was almost overshadowed by Freddie and Wayne. But he was able compose and write—and he knew how to write for the Jazz Messengers."

Walton was thrilled with the process in which the band collectively developed their original compositions. "We'd put six, seven, eight songs together—and they wouldn't be short [songs], because we were a sextet, and we all soloed extensively—then we'd go in and record them." But what thrilled him even more was that his bandmates just nailed the tunes. "Wayne, Freddie, and Curtis stand out as the most immediate interpreters of charts that I've ever played with. I tried to play 'Mosaic' when I was with the Jazztet; we must've played it fifty times, and we never could get it. But when I brought it to the Messengers, they played it the first time around. They burnt me on my own song; I said, 'I'd better brush up on this.' They ate it for breakfast. When Art added his touch, it wouldn't take us long to get pieces down."

With an exotic, Eastern-sounding fourteen-bar "A" section drifting into a syncopated sixteen-bar "B" section, it's understandable why the fleet "Mosaic" was tabbed as the disc's title cut. Seemingly ready-made for the Messengers, the song proclaimed the arrival of a vital composer—not just for the Jazz Messengers, but also for the jazz world in general.

In terms of quantity, Walton picked his spots, throwing a tune into the till only when it was spot on. "Shaky Jake" (*Buhaina's Delight*, Blue Note, 1961) is a lazy shuffling blues with a bridge, festive in its mid-tempo simplicity. A kissing cousin to "Mosaic," "Plexis" (*Three Blind Mice*, Blue Note,

1962) is a microcosm of what would ultimately become Walton's mature compositional method, characterized by taut harmonies, shifting styles, and hip unison piano and bass lines. Cedar's most celebrated tune, though, is the title cut of *Ugetsu*, a.k.a. "Fantasy in 'D'." At once harmonious and intense, the lighthearted effort pendulums between a vamp-based swing section and a pedal-point-based interlude that Hubbard, Shorter, Fuller, and Walton navigate lusciously.

Solo-wise, the majority of Walton's improvs were also luscious, a fact that Cedar credits in part to Buhaina himself. "Art would drive us from the rear, drive us like he was a carriage and we were a team of horses. The pianist, at least when I was with him, really had to be strong; you had to time your playing to be heard over his powerful style. It was when I joined Blakey that I started gaining power and strength." It was a must that Cedar crank up his volume so he could both supplement and compete with his leader. "My playing got stronger, because with Art's powerful style I had to get stronger. But [Blakey's volume] was deceptive—he would leave little cracks for you. He had a real keen sense of radar, especially from the piano standpoint. A trumpeter could overcome Art's volume—well, actually, sometimes I had my doubts about that—but the pianist had to develop that radar so he could get in there and find the holes. And Art would leave the holes, because he was an ex-piano player. I learned how to play during the milliseconds he wasn't playing."

Benny Green felt that even though Walton held his own power-wise, he was always more about brains than brawn. "I always loved Cedar's economy, how he was able to say so much with so few notes, and use a lot of space. He really has the inside track on accompaniment. I would say his sound, his use of register, and his unique time feel were elements that I really tried to embrace when I was with Art. It was very much a part of connecting with Art, calling upon this language. There were certain beats that Art played that just reeked of Cedar Walton." (Even non-pianists were affected by Walton's feel. "Cedar's touch was one of the really individual things about him," Brian Lynch said, "the hornlike way he plays. His phrasing has been influential to me.")

Shorter's "Contemplation" is the lone ballad on the lively *Buhaina's Delight*; Walton's chorus on the tune is a blur of double- and triple-time runs that, while technically stellar, never compromise the atmosphere of Wayne's tone poem. "His solo on 'Contemplation' off of *Buhania's Delight* is beautiful," Steve Davis said. "It sounds like it was recorded yesterday." His chorus on the bossa "Pensitiva" (*Free for All*) is another picture-perfect work of art, a collection of single-note runs and block chords that gives life to the song's title.

The pianist never took anything for granted during his three years as a Jazz Messenger. "It was really a great time for us. We were encouraged to learn how to be leaders, and Art was a good model for us. He was good at programming the pieces we played, and he was good with audiences. And I think we all inherited that. We were a group that had a whole lot of fun. It was non-stop—whenever we thought we were going to have a day off, Art would call us and say, 'Let's go.'"

Cedar Walton answered Art Blakey's call to arms.

Cedar Walton *went*.

BELONGING
Keith Jarrett

"Keith Jarrett is a very sensitive, very expert player."
—Cedar Walton

WHEN YOU THINK "Keith Jarrett," you think "esoteric long-form improvisations," you think "meditative classical-based compositions," you think "jazz deconstructionism." What you don't think is "hard bop." For that matter, you don't think "soft bop." Heck, you don't think "bop" of any kind whatsoever.

In light of his eventual wide-ranging career path, it's pretty darn weird to think of Keith Jarrett as a Jazz Messenger, a fact undisputed by Art Blakey. "It was really a misfit," Buhaina said bluntly. But the supposed lack of connection stemmed not from a shortage of aptitude on Jarrett's part, but rather from an overabundance of talent. Blakey continued, "The reason why things were so terribly unbalanced there was [because] Keith was a very accomplished musician and there were other musicians in the band who were growing. Sometimes a man has so much talent he would get bored waiting for the rest of the cats to catch up. And Keith could play other instruments too, so he knew what the saxophone player was doing wrong, what the trumpet player was doing wrong. He was in the band because of me, because he liked me. But it's like a kid in school—put him in the wrong class and he gets bored."

Only twenty-one when he joined the group in 1966, the wise-beyond-his-years pianist was well aware of the realities of his situation. "It wasn't very easy for me to play with Blakey because, being a drummer myself, I had a conception completely opposed to his, and it was a constant struggle." But struggle often breeds fine art, a maxim exemplified by Jarrett's only recording with the Messengers, *Buttercorn Lady*.

"I love how Keith played on *Buttercorn Lady*," Mulgrew Miller raved. "He was dealing with a wider palette than his predecessors in the band. He brought his whole impressionistic, free, atonal leanings to the band. He brought a certain level of agility."

The pianist's dexterity—not to mention his indisputable musicality—is displayed on the standard ballad "My Romance." On this feature for Chuck Mangione, Jarrett's two choruses are laden with floaty rhythms and quirky, somewhat dissonant double-, triple-, and quadruple-time runs. And then there's his solo on "Recuerdo," which is possibly the most bizarre Messenger solo in the history of Messenger solos. Aside from the fact that it's far more dissonant than his spot in "My Romance," and aside from the fact that he places his notes in between the in betweens of a beat—places where Messengers don't normally place notes—the dude spends about half of his lengthy improv plucking and pushing the piano strings. In spite of his frustration with his pianist, Blakey nonetheless good-naturedly goaded Jarrett to engage in that sort of envelope pushing. "Whenever Keith would do something like [strumming the strings]," Mangione related, "Art would encourage him by yelling, 'Act like a fool!' And Keith did, because Keith is Keith. He was as unique then as he is now."

Blakey gave Donald Brown a special insight regarding Jarrett's standing in the band. "I love *Buttercorn Lady*, but I always hear it in a different light, just because I remember talking to Bu about it. Bu would say, 'Keith was a great player, but he had so many problems—he was always bugging me about firing the other guys in the band, because they weren't on his level.' To me, everyone in that band meant business, but you hear Keith, and you know he was a notch above—even then, he was playing on a level above everyone else. Bu also told me that Keith played a little bass, and he would take the bassist's instrument and play something on it, then he'd pick up a saxophone and do the same thing. Art said that was because he didn't really know who he was. But Art thought he could play the hell out of the piano. I'm thankful he did that one record. To hear him in a context like that, you know that he definitely paid his dues. He knows the music."

Jarrett is as far removed from Silver, Timmons, et al., as Art Blakey is from, say, Led Zeppelin's John Bonham. One of the only Messengers instrumentalists to almost fully diverge from the hard bop trail blazed by his forerunners, Keith nonetheless made an impression on his heirs apparent. And while his unconventional vision didn't directly affect the subsequent generation of Messengers pianists, Keith Jarrett proved that Buhaina had big ears, a big heart, and a big sense of open-mindedness—all qualities that contributed to the range and longevity of the Jazz Messengers.

UNLIMITED
James Williams

"James Williams played a pivotal role in the Jazz Messengers' history. He's an avid student of the music, and helped keep the band alive during a questionable time."

—Benny Green

JAMES WILLIAMS is one of the most humble musicians of the modern jazz era—that is, until the discussion turns to his alleged physical beauty. "Before I got hired, Art was looking for a good-looking piano player," James claimed. "I was the obvious choice."

Handsomeness aside, Williams—along with Bobby Watson, Valery Ponomarev, and David Schnitter—was one of the Messengers' saviors in the bumpy 1970s, a fact confirmed by Benny Green: "It was really a rarity at that point for young pianists to be playing acoustic piano, playing straight-ahead jazz. He set the stage for the rest of the Messenger pianists, and I don't think he gets enough credit for that. It was so important to me as a young person like me to go see James play with the band, and realize firsthand that there was a sense of a continuum [in the band], that this was something that young people could pick up on and be a part of."

From the get-go, Green gleaned that Williams was ushering in a new era. "The first time I saw James with the band, I was impressed at how much he'd clearly absorbed of the history and the spectrum of the music, but he had a feeling that was contemporary and personal. The warmth of his feeling and the color of his music really had a deep impact on me. He made the notion of playing with Art a reality."

The twenty-five-year-old Memphis, Tennessee, native was welcomed into the Messengers fold in 1977 not just because of what he knew, but also because of whom he knew. "I was recommended by [pianist] George Cables and [bassist] Dennis Irwin," Williams said. "George had heard me sit in with Freddie Hubbard. Art was looking for a young pianist who was a composer and arranger, so I guess George thought I filled the bill."

Though his effervescent pianistic approach filled said bill to a T, Williams was nonetheless hungry to do more than merely fit in. "The Messengers gave me the opportunity to play with excellent musicians, to play some of the more prestigious clubs and concert halls, to travel around the world and grow up, to arrange and compose pieces for the band, and to record. Plus, we were playing five or six nights a week on average; we would tour over nine months a year. He provided me with a forum to experiment— as he did for all the previous editions of the Jazz Messengers. It was like a workshop-in-progress. I tried to take advantage of all those facets."

His musical voice was well on its way to being established before he became a Messenger, but the nightly work accelerated James's musical growth immeasurably. Williams's earliest sessions with the band spotlight a nimble, hyper-vigorous keyboardist eager to excite and charm. His florid rubato intro to the standard "The Song Is You" (*In This Korner*) is potent in its depth—or possibly deep in its potency—and is the ideal launching pad for the brisk rave-up. And his chorus on his original blues-soaked shuffle "Reflections in Blue" (*In My Prime, 1*) is one of those everything-including-the-kitchen-sink solos, a stunning exhibition of chops and complexity. But three years later, James had widened his palette to include some more muted colors: "My Romance," his feature tune on *Straight Ahead*, exudes the kind of broad humor and wide dynamic range that characterized Williams's fully mature style.

Mulgrew Miller, another Memphis man who first started palling around with Williams in the late 1970s, noted that Williams is as versatile as versatile can be, both a killer pianist and a killer composer. "James is a very talented and a very astute musician, one who's well versed in harmony and the jazz repertoire. Because of his harmonic probing, his piano playing sometimes transcended the players that came before him. All of that helps to make for a very broad musician. He also is a fine composer. The [Messengers] groups that James was in helped the band's resurgence—it was the beginning of the youthful renaissance of the band. While his compositions had a soulful flavor in the tradition of the band, because of James's broad harmonic sense, he added a new tonal color to the band's sound. His tunes helped bring a new sleekness and slickness to the Messengers."

"When you brought in a composition," Williams said, "you had to know the Jazz Messengers' sound; you had to know Art Blakey's sound if you wanted to have your pieces played. When you wrote for that band, you couldn't just say, 'Oh, I happen to have some arrangements at the house, I'll just bring 'em in.' But if you *did* do that, you had to be flexible, and know how to bend and let it work in that context. One thing about the Jazz Messengers, no matter what the personnel was, the band sounded like the Jazz Messengers."

"Soulful Mr. Timmons" (*Album of the Year*) is a textbook example of Williams's ability to capture that elusive sound. Another blues-rooted shuffle, the tune doesn't resemble one of Bobby's tunes per se, but, as James noted, the Timmons vibe was most definitely in the house. "'Soulful Mr. Timmons' was very characteristic of the Jazz Messengers. As the melody was starting to come to fruition and take shape, I said, 'Boy, this sounds like Bobby's personality.' So it named itself, in a sense; once I completed the idea, it was obvious what the title should be."

James cherished the edition of the band heard on *Straight Ahead* and *Album of the Year* not just for the way they brought his tunes to life, but because they injected life into Buhaina himself. "When we had Billy Pierce, Bobby Watson, Wynton Marsalis, Charles Fambrough, and myself, we realized that we had something special because we could see an attitude adjustment with Art. He was more enthusiastic. He always loved to play—he'd go to jam sessions even after concerts—but I could hear him playing with a kind of intensity that I hadn't noticed in the previous editions of the band. It helped when this band came together, we had three guys on the front line who had a real love for playing ensembles, who knew how to phrase, knew all the nuances. I think it was also the excitement of having a young guy like Wynton.

"But Art wasn't just a magnet for young musicians—a lot of the masters would come by and hang around. I remember [drummer] Billy Higgins and Max Roach getting off of a plane in transit, just so they could see Art. Dizzy Gillespie, [drummer] Roy Haynes, Gary Bartz, [drummer] Bernard Purdie, [trumpeter] Blue Mitchell—so many different people came by to sit in. [Comedian] Redd Foxx would come by. [Author] James Baldwin came to Mikell's two or three times. Art invited him up to the stage just to acknowledge him, and James spoke to the audience. That was a thrill. I knew they weren't coming out to see James Williams—they didn't know who I was."

The headiness of Messengerdom was invaluable to Williams in terms of his personal development. "It helped me to learn some life lessons, being able to make decisions about my life and career—and to be able to live with those decisions, for better or for worse. Art didn't hold classes on life lessons; he taught through example. In a sense, we were improvisers off the stage, too. I'd be thinking: *Do I want to do this? Do I want to do that? Do I want to hang out late tonight? What are my responsibilities back home? When am I going to get a chance to practice? When am I going to get to write arrangements? Will we play the arrangements when I write them? How will I adjust to traveling this frequently?* These kinds of things were largely foreign to most of us. In a situation like that, you almost need to be a young person. You need to learn all of this while you're young when you're open to more ideas, and you're not thinking, *Oh, gosh, I wish I was at home because so-and-so is there, and I'd really rather just go see movies.* We didn't get into that lazy, lazy mentality. We wanted to be out and be on the scene every night, because we might miss something if we weren't there."

Williams is both proud and conflicted that the Messenger tag will be with him forever. "Guys that played with Art had that same out-of-body experience—no matter how accomplished we became, this Jazz Messenger legacy is going to follow us everywhere. Often, when I see a biography of mine, the first thing they almost always say is that I played with the Jazz Messengers. Many times [before a concert] they'll introduce me as 'former Jazz Messenger piano player James Williams,' as if my career has been in a state of suspended animation [since then]. I've been blessed to play with Elvin Jones, Art Farmer, Milt Jackson, Benny Carter, and I've had two good groups of my own. But the Jazz Messengers is in many cases what gets mentioned. And I don't have any problem with that, because we are all—and always will be—Jazz Messengers."

SWEETEST SOUNDS
Donald Brown

"Donald Brown is a genius. That's a term that's overused, but in this particular case, it's probably an understatement."

—James Williams

ART BLAKEY may have baptized the bulk of his recruits by fire, but Donald Brown's indoctrination was tempered with a smidgen of ice. "My second week with the band, we were playing Blues Alley in Washington, D.C.," Brown said. "After the first or second night, we had a little meeting, then after the meeting was done, Art had me stick around for a few minutes. He said, 'I really like the way you play, and I really like the way you comp, but you just need to relax, because you seem uptight. Just relax, because you don't have nothin' to prove to nobody—you're up here with me. Those people in the audience, the fact that you're up here with me, that makes them think you're great. You only have to do one thing, and that's swing *me* into the ground.'"

During his two stints with the Messengers, the pianist followed Buhaina's directive. But the Memphis native wouldn't have had the chance to swing Blakey into the ground if it weren't for a certain special someone who hailed from Brown's hometown. "James Williams is like my best friend, he's like my mentor," Donald said. "He's like my manager—he's just a beautiful individual. He's put me before himself so many times, I know I wouldn't have accomplished as much as I have without him. When he was getting ready to leave [the Messengers], he informed me that there was going to be an opening in the band and wanted to know if I'd be interested in auditioning.

"It was sort of strange," Brown continued, "because before I [auditioned for the Messengers], I was playing with a Top 40 band, and James got a tape to the band of me playing some of my [pop-oriented] compositions. James had also recommended me to audition with Clark Terry and people like that, but I turned them down, because at the time, I didn't think I was strong enough. I think when James got ready to leave Bu, I knew I'd better audition, because if I didn't try out for something, James was going to think, 'Well, Donald's going to always feel he's not good enough, and I won't call him anymore.' So I tried out. I ended up doing the audition with three other pianists. I can't even remember if Art was at the audition or not; Bobby

Watson and Billy Pierce were there. I felt pretty prepared in the sense that I was studying the [Messengers'] music pretty heavily—I knew most of the book before I joined. The first time I was in the band in 1981, I was there for roughly one year. Then I rejoined the band in 1986 for seven or eight months."

Brown's pen was as mighty, if not mightier, than his keyboard, and he instantly made his writing presence felt. Mulgrew Miller, the third member of the Messenger Memphis mob, recognized the Williams-to-Brown compositional continuum. "Donald brought James's characteristics to the highest level, in terms of his writing contribution. He was probably the most masterful composer that took the piano chair in many a year."

"My compositional concept was definitely developing before I joined the band," Donald said. "The compositions I first brought to the band, I'd written before I had any idea I'd be joining Art. The first tune I brought in, I'd written it with a drummer in mind, and it worked out great—that was 'New York.' But it took on a different shape and grew a lot more with the band."

With its chunk-style harmonies and outrageously complex ensemble passages, "New York" (*Live: New Year's Eve at Sweet Basil*, ProJazz Records, 1986) could have been cowritten by fellow Messenger compositional heavies Walter Davis Jr. and Bobby Watson. "'New York' is a classic," Williams said. "Donald is a major composer, easily the premier of our generation writing in this style. He's something to behold. He brought a dimension that helped unify the band's sound with the Marsalis brothers."

At first listen, Brown's writing style has more in common with the modern Messengers composers, but his prime influence was an old-school scribe. "I found myself trying to emulate Cedar Walton's compositional style, his sophistication," Donald explained. "Subconsciously, I'd think, 'How would Cedar do that?' But then Art would be pushing me, saying, 'You've got to think about being yourself.' But it was really hard to get that sound, and that standard out of my ear."

While self-assured about the quality of his songs, Donald was initially tentative on the keys. "One of my biggest concerns when I joined the band was to get my sound together so I could project. When you think about Horace, and Bobby Timmons, and Cedar, and you think about the other guys, [projecting] was a big part of it.

"I can remember when we were doing some arrangement of mine, and Art said, 'Your chords need some weight to them.' I wasn't sure what he was talking about, but then he sat at the piano and demonstrated, and he showed me that I could just play the root and the fifth, which would make it more of a traditional voicing. I would have done that normally in other contexts, but in this particular situation, I didn't think that's what I needed to do. Art was a helluva piano player, and he got his message across loud and clear—it was like a piano lesson for me. I realized he had a wisdom, and so many ways of getting it across. He had a way of instructing without saying anything—I'd just learn by watching him, how he directed the band, how he'd pace the soloists and the song itself, and his use of dynamics. I realized I had to work hard, and the ultimate goal was to be swinging."

As Brown gravitated toward the compositional end of the musical spectrum, it stood to reason that some of his most interesting piano playing wasn't of the improvised variety, but rather the interpreted. His intro to Thelonious Monk's "In Walked Bud" (*Keystone 3*) is a tempo-less rundown of the melody's "A" section, a glittery reading that would have brought a grin to Monk's face. To that end, the outro—a slowed-down reprise of the intro—actually elicited some chuckles from the live audience, owing to the fact that he never resolves the melody, leaving the crowd on the edge of their seats.

Sidemanning for Art Blakey gave Donald Brown the credibility necessary to land heaps of high-profile jazz gigs, but Brown viewed the Jazz Messengers as much more than a springboard. "With all the people I've played with—Freddie Hubbard, Johnny Griffin, Eddie 'Lockjaw' Davis—I still consider this the highlight of my career. Art was close to the source of the beginning of the music. That's why there was so much growing that took place."

WINGSPAN
Mulgrew Miller

"Mulgrew Miller has such enthusiasm—every time he sits down at the piano, he's like a kid that's been given this gift. He's the most complete pianist of my generation."

—Donald Brown

"MULGREW MILLER is a state-of-the-art pianist," James Williams gushed. "There may be others who have more lucrative record contracts with major record companies, there may be others who are the flavor of the month, but when all the dust clears, the one that's really standing tall—both figuratively and literally—is Mulgrew. He towers over all of us in terms of what he brings to the table: The intangibles, that he can uplift, that he can make his bandmates play better than they would otherwise play. It truly is Miller time when he's on the bandstand."

James may be biased—after all, as noted, the keyboardists both hail from Memphis, Tennessee—but his declaration is far from an overstatement. A player whose remarkable melodicism and awe-inspiring chops are so ingrained as to seem second nature, Mulgrew Miller imposed his musical will on the Jazz Messengers between 1984 and 1986.

Considering his relationship with fellow Volunteer State-ers/ex-Messengers Williams and Donald Brown, it was all but inevitable that Miller would hook up with Blakey. "Mulgrew Miller came to Memphis State University the year after I started," Donald said. "James, Mulgrew, and I would get together in the music building, pull three pianos together, and just play. That was a great learning experience—three different minds approaching the same tune. Needless to say, there was a lot of sharing of ideas going on."

After college, Mulgrew had little trouble entrenching himself into the international jazz scene, quickly landing sideman gigs with the Duke Ellington Big Band, Woody Shaw, and vocalist Betty Carter—all of which led him to Messengerland. "I would see Art here and there while I was on the road with Betty and Woody, so he was aware of me," Miller said. "Terence Blanchard and Donald Harrison were in the Messengers at the time, and I had been working with them on some of their own gigs, so when [pianist] Johnny O'Neal left the band and the piano chair became vacant, I was recommended by Terence and Donald. My meeting with Art Blakey was an interesting experience. I was told to go by his house to talk to him—I guess you could call it my interview—and what was interesting was that he never asked me to join the band. He just told me where the next gig was, and what time to be there."

For Miller, the Messenger wheels moved quickly, but despite his extensive professional experience, he flailed for a brief while. "'When I joined the band, I was the oldest guy there, and I was already a mature adult by then—but I was forced to be more musically extroverted than I'd ever been. I can remember that first month, not feeling very comfortable; I knew the band's 'hits,' but I only had a couple of weeks to learn the other things. By the time I was in the band, Art was losing his hearing. Sometimes the beat would be unsettled, and that was kind of unnerving. Also, with other groups, I always felt I needed to direct the rhythm section, pianistically; with my comping, I thought I could pull the rhythm section along. But I quickly found out that you can't lead Art—I found that out *fast*. Along with all that, Art had such a big beat, and he would play those in-between tempos that Monk used to play, so it took me a minute to get used to that." But get used to it he did, and he didn't merely find his niche in the band—he thrived. "My playing just generally matured. I don't think one single characteristic changed, but the experience certainly boosted my confidence. It brought me out a little bit more—a general budding, if you will."

According to Joanne Brackeen, Miller's blossoming was manifest. "Mulgrew has to be one of the sweetest players. He can play with anybody; he can play old-style, he can play modern-style. *Very* creative." That creativity is evident throughout the Jackie McLean–penned title cut of *Dr. Jeckyle* (ProJazz Records, 1985). On this manic twelve-bar blues, Miller spits out a string of harmonically challenging right-hand runs, his imaginative note choices never overshadowing his sense of melody.

Oh, yeah—Mr. Miller could also write. "Mulgrew's a very fine composer," Williams said. "He doesn't get enough credit for his composing, but he really does have some wonderful pieces."

An unabashed admirer of Mulgrew's writing, Cedar Walton agreed with Williams. "He wrote this one song, 'Second Thoughts,' and I had to compliment him on the structure of the tune. It had *everything*: question and answer, dynamics, and it fit the band perfectly. I can't say enough about his talent."

Walton nailed it on the head—unselfconscious in its Messenger-ness, the relaxed "Second Thoughts" (*Coast to Coast*) is a twenty-four-bar tune oozing Benny Golson's singability and Wayne Shorter's chordal convolution.

Like Billy Pierce, Miller is a musician's musician, hugely respected by his piano-playing peers. "Mulgrew has been a role model for me because of his mastery and finesse," Benny Green said. "He's the consummate polished young master of the piano. He has the most exquisite touch of his generation. I watched Mulgrew very closely with the Messengers—how he handled himself, how he negotiated playing behind the different soloists—and I really admired his approach to playing with Art. Mulgrew had already established his beautiful touch and sound, all of which he didn't compromise when he joined the Messengers. There's so much power going on up there [playing with Blakey] that someone like myself, I oftentimes had to play the piano as physically hard as I could to project. Mulgrew took much more of a Teddy Wilson or Hank Jones approach, where if you want to open up your sound, do it through orchestration rather than velocity. He showed so much maturity and finesse when he played with the Messengers."

"Mulgrew is one of my best friends," Brown said. "When I first met him, I'd go hear him play, and he'd be playing all this fast, incredible stuff, and it was so incredible that it used to piss me off. He's had the perfect career: He started out with the Ellington band, he played with Betty, he played with Woody, he played with Bu. He played in a big band, he played behind a singer, he played in small group situations, and I always tell him that that's why he's one the most recorded pianists of this era. Before I go and do a recording, I'll listen to him just to see what's up. He can play the hell out of a ballad, he can play loud music, any tempo, any key. He has a big sound, and you can hear a lot of warmth and humility in his playing.

"That's Mulgrew—he's a gentleman."

NATURALLY
Benny Green

"Benny Green could be the monster pianist of the twenty-first century."

—Joanne Brackeen

TIME AND AGAIN, Art Blakey declared that he preferred to fill his band with young, raw recruits, if only because playing with the kids kept him fresh. But here's the thing: That also worked in reverse. Whether it was Blakey's drumming, his conception, or his charisma, youthful jazz up-and-comers gravitated toward the Jazz Messengers; musicians would rather join forces with Blakey than gig with their contemporaries, because the Messengers were eternally inventive within their established hard bop framework.

Benny Green was the paradigm for neophyte instrumentalists who were determined to be a Jazz Messenger.

Green was a mere tot of seventeen when he was seduced by Buhaina's aggregation. "I'd go hear the band every time they were in town," the California-born keyboardist said, "and I'd tape them on my little Walkman so I could learn the entire repertoire. I would literally eat, sleep, and breathe the Jazz Messengers. I'd sleep with my Walkman on, listening to one of my live tapes, or one of their records, and practice exclusively with those recordings. In so doing, hopefully I was absorbing some of the feel. After having seen the band with James Williams and Donald Brown, respectively, at that point I knew I was going to move to New York with very specific aspirations to play with Art."

Soon after the nineteen-year-old Green alighted in the Big Apple in 1982, he sought out Williams, who took the eager youngster under his sizable wings. "Benny used to come over to my house and ask a lot of questions and play a lot of records and tape my albums," James said. "He was always very interested in learning; he wanted to know how to play everything the right way. He might have been too academic in that approach, but that's part of the learning curve. He has literally transformed himself into an excellent musician through the sheer power of his will and his discipline—which is what all of us should strive toward."

Benny's initial meeting with Buhaina was less than auspicious. "The pianist in the Messengers at that time was Johnny O'Neal, and we became friends. One day Johnny asked me, 'Benny, how would you like to play with this band?' I told him, 'Johnny, there's nothing I'd like more in the whole world.' He said, 'Well, let me introduce you to Art.' Even though that was one of the main focuses of moving to New York—to meet Art, to play with the Messengers—I was somehow terrified of actually meeting him. He was larger than life to me, an icon. After we were introduced, Art looked at me up and down, from head to toe. I had medium-to-long hair, and I was wearing a plaid work shirt, blue jeans, and sneakers—I was fresh off the banana boat. After he gave me a thorough once-over, he said, 'How long ya been in town?' I said, 'Six weeks.' He looked me over again, then he said, 'Ya need more time.' It's like I was a fish that he was throwing back into the water. But I knew that he was right, and I didn't feel slighted."

Like pianist John Hicks and Mulgrew Miller before him, Green apprenticed with singer Betty Carter before connecting with Blakey. "I worked with Betty for four years, and even though I wanted to play with Art, I'm so glad I had a chance to work with Betty. I don't think I would've been able to hang in with the Messengers if I hadn't gotten all that experience that she gave me. She was tough, and I was thankful for it. You had to learn how to play in any key at any tempo. She insisted on total creativity; if she heard you play something one night, she would just about fire you if you played it the next night. When I joined the Messengers in 1986, I thought I'd had a little bit of experience—which I did—but it was such a new thing playing with Art; in terms of the power and shape he would give each performance, it was almost overwhelming." (Williams agreed that it was a blessing for Green to have gigged with Carter. "It was lucky for him that he had had a chance to play with Betty before he came into the Jazz Messengers; if he hadn't had that, I think he could have been totally overwhelmed.")

Armed with his newfound wisdom, Green was well prepared the second time he met Blakey, confident, ready, and raring to go. "Word was out in New York that Donald Brown was going to be leaving the band, and that Art would be looking for a new pianist. When I went down to Sweet Basil's to sit in, it seemed like all the young pianists in the city were there—even Harry Connick Jr. was there. When Art brought me up to the bandstand, he called a tune that you either knew or you didn't—Walter Davis's 'Uranus.' Fortunately, I knew it. I'd been practicing that song, waiting for that moment. After the set was over, Art said, 'I want you to come back tomorrow night.' So I went back, and what did he have me play? 'Uranus' again. I think he really dug hearing me play that song for some reason, because after that, he hired me."

Thanks to "Uranus," the gig was his, but it wasn't long before Blakey plunked Green right on the hot seat. "Pretty much every single night, he'd have me play an extensive solo feature. Doing that in the context of a Jazz Messengers show, that was a real trial by fire for me. To have Art walk off the bandstand—and to have to fill up that void of him being gone—that really helped me in a big way to develop my sound and feeling playing solo piano. That was a huge gift."

His extended unaccompanied solos were challenging, but improvising in the ensemble setting was a joy, exhilarating partly due to the rapport he shared with his leader. "There was nothing like the way Art would play behind a piano solo, whether he would go to brushes or if he got that circular motion going on the ride cymbal. I realized that there was an axis that existed between the pianists and Art's drumming—there was a very definite language there. Art would set up a real flavor to my solo, right from the beginning. That was a wonderful feeling. It was terrific to play with a drummer who took such pride in setting you a place at the table. You would have had to be a stone to not feel inspired to play with Art behind you." Blakey also aided Green with his behind-the-soloist accompaniment. "Art would just lock his eyes with me and we'd comp together. He had a strong visual connection with the pianist that was unbreakable. He transmitted so much positive energy into you.

"Whatever instrument you played with Art," Green continued, "you had a choice of developing your sound so you could project in the context of his drums, or just getting completely steamrolled. An element in my personality—it's my Aries nature, perhaps—makes that the kind of challenge I love to rise to. My [physical] build at the time I joined the band was so slight—I was a really tiny little guy—and to hold the piano chair with the Messengers, you had to really be able to project. However big your sound was, Art would give that sound a lot of depth and color. One thing that Mulgrew Miller and I shared during our respective experiences with the Messengers was that Art would give so much shape to your solo that he created the illusion that this power was coming from you. He would be playing you, in effect. You'd be thinking, 'Wow, my sound is really developing,' and then you'd go and play a gig with another drummer, and you'd feel like someone just pulled the rug out from under you."

If he'd had his druthers, Benny would have elected himself Messenger-pianist-for-life, thus for him, leaving the band was bittersweet—especially in light of the circumstances surrounding his departure. "I didn't quit the band—Art fired me. I knew I wasn't going to quit the band—I was so happy playing with Art. But [bassist] Peter Washington said, 'You'd better leave, Benny. You've gotta do Art before he does you.' I said I really didn't care, I just wanted to continue playing with him. I was a little naïve, because if I wasn't going to quit, I was going to be fired. I was sort of in denial. But Art was like a vampire, he really thrived on new young blood. What was really harsh for me is that I thought that if Art did fire me—I wasn't going to quit, remember—we would have this beautiful long talk where I would be gracious and thank Art for bringing me into the band, for teaching me, and for allowing me to grow. But that's not what happened. What happened was the European road manager called me only a week prior to a tour and said, 'When we go over to England, Geoffrey Keezer's going to be doing the tour.' It was hard not to hear it from Art, and to not have that closure. I left the band really angry with Art. I wanted to thank him, but I wasn't given that opportunity. He booted me out of the nest, which made me determined to *do it*, to succeed on my own."

Fortunately, Green reconciled with Buhaina—which was no surprise, considering that he was predisposed to love Art Blakey, to love being a Jazz Messenger. It was that love that compelled him to draw upon Buhaina's well of knowledge every time he touches a piano. "Finding my voice was so interlinked with playing with Art; it's a process I'll continue to go through as I live my life playing music."

TURN UP THE QUIET
Geoffrey Keezer

"Geoffrey Keezer has a flair for playing all over the piano. His facility is the most outstanding thing about him."

—Cedar Walton

IN ONE MANNER or another, each and every Jazz Messenger matured during his Blakey years. For some, the maturation took the form of musical development, while for others, it was all about personal growth.

For Geoffrey Keezer, it was about growing *old*. "I played with the Jazz Messengers for one year, and I think I aged about ten years in that one year. I went from being a naïve Midwestern Wisconsin boy to being a crusty New Yorker."

Like his piano-chair predecessor Benny Green, Geoffrey Keezer—who joined the band in 1989 at age nineteen—was all but fated to be a Messenger. "I felt like I fit in right away, because since I was about fourteen years old, it was a goal of mine to be in the band," Keezer said. "I had already learned all the music. I actually had a band in high school that played some Messenger tunes, so I was thoroughly familiar with their repertoire."

As was the case with Donald Brown and Benny Green, it was James Williams who facilitated Keezer's entrée into the group. "I was going to Berklee College of Music in 1988," Geoffrey said. "I had met James a few years before that. I had been corresponding with James, sending him tapes of my music. When I got to Berklee, I would take the train from Boston to New York whenever I had a little extra cash. I would always stay with James at his apartment in Brooklyn, and he would take me club-hopping. Through him, I met a lot of older musicians who were heroes of mine. One night, James took me up to Mikell's, where Art was playing. He talked to Art and said, 'You should hear this guy,' so Art let me sit in. I played the last two songs of the set with the band—I think one of the tunes was Horace Silver's 'Mayreh.' Art liked what I did, and several months later, he came up to Boston with the band, and I sat in again. After the set, Art walked up to me and said, 'Give me your Social Security number.' I think he wanted to hire me at that point, but he didn't call until September of 1989—which was when I moved to New York after one year at Berklee. It was perfect timing, because I got the call to join the group basically when I moved to New York."

As usual, Williams's talent scouting was on target. "I sensed—as did Art— Geoffrey's prodigious talent," Williams said. He'd absorbed so much of the history of jazz piano, whether you're talking about Bud Powell and Art Tatum, or Herbie Hancock and McCoy Tyner. Dr. K is a little guy, but he knows how to get the sound out of the keyboard, because he's so fundamentally sound." (Keezer pointed out that his forceful dynamic level was born out of necessity. "Being with the band made me a physically stronger player," Geoffrey said. "It made me play a lot harder, and it took me years to undo that. Art played so loud, and we never used stage monitors, so I really had to bang the piano in order to hear myself.")

While it was essential that he bang in a live setting, in the studio Keezer was able to utilize a broader dynamic spectrum. On his blithe arrangement of Billy Strayhorn's "Raincheck" (*Chippin' In*), his one solo chorus—filled with jangly, discordant, Monk-ish runs—is understated and contemplative, two qualities he likely didn't get a chance to employ on stage.

That final edition of the band was a septet, and four of its members liked to compose, so in the spirit of democracy, each writer was allowed to contribute a song or three to the Messengers book. "Brain Stormin'" (*Chippin' In*), Keezer's lone recorded tune with the band, is a non-standard A-A-B-A-formatted mid-tempo groover; the "A" section is dissonant but still melodic and memorable, while the bridge is a fresh, syncopated Latin interlude.

Like his bandmates Brian Lynch and Javon Jackson, Keezer was the ideal musician for Buhaina's final ensemble. While he was on track to establishing his own voice, he was right in the Messengers tradition, but with one eye gazing into the future — and in Geoffrey's mind, there was no other way to go. "If you're playing jazz with a band like Art Blakey and the Jazz Messengers, you can't avoid being in the tradition—by its very nature it's a traditional kind of band. He had an ability to open up your sound, no matter what instrument you played. He was three times my age, but it was hard to keep up with him."

Even Benny Green—who was exceptionally bummed out by the manner in which the transition from himself to Keezer was handled—believed his replacement was a more than worthy successor. "Geoffrey is able to play so much piano with apparent ease," Green said. "He's really a natural pianist. As difficult as it was for me to accept being fired personally, musically it was very clear that Geoffrey brought something to the plate. He has a quiet virtuosity. He's able to communicate without a show of force. The music just flows from him."

PIANO NOTES

ONE OF THE most unsung of the unsung Messenger heroes, **Sam Dockery** was yet *another* one of those ubiquitous Philly-born Messengers phenomena. While his style wasn't particularly Messenger-like—think Horace Silver minus the funk—he was a stabilizing force for the 1956–57 Jackie McLean/Bill Hardman band, if only because his improvs were cool breezes in the midst of the horn-rooted heat wave. His lone compositional contribution to the band, "Sam's Tune" (*Ritual*, Blue Note, 1957), is a solid modal-based burner that made you wish he'd put pen to paper a helluva lot more often.

Though he was with the Jazz Messengers for only a relatively brief time, **John Hicks**'s two fleeting stints with the band—1964–65 and 1972–73—changed him forever. "Art was pretty heavy on piano players. There were tons of tunes to learn and Art wouldn't allow any music on the bandstand. He said you were supposed to remember it. Art just sort of pushed me out there and said, 'You got it.' Of course once I got into it I saw how great it was."

"When I had **Joanne Brackeen** in the band," Art Blakey said, "we were playing down South. This was in Georgia or somewhere. This guy came up and said, 'Hey there, Mr. Blakey. You know, you got a white gal in the band!' I said, 'No shit, I have to check it out. I thought I had a piano player!'"

In one of the most unstable periods in Jazz Messengers history, Joanne Brackeen was a steadying force; between 1970 and 1972, the Messengers were somewhat of a revolving door, and though the piano chair was periodically up for grabs, Brackeen was the rock.

Joanne's induction into the group was positively serendipitous. "The Messengers were playing at Slugs in New York City. I lived right around the corner in a sixth-floor walk-up, and I had four kids; so for me to go out was a big deal. I was just kinda spacing out one night, so I went around the corner to hear him, and the band just sounded great. The piano player wasn't playing, but it sounded to me like there should've been piano in there, and I guess I must've known the tune they were playing, because I walked up to the pianist and said, 'Do you mind if I play?' The guy said, 'Go ahead.' I just took over in the middle of the tune. Art looked up after the set was over, and saw a different face at the piano. Then I was hired a couple of days later."

Mulgrew Miller had much love for the pianist who directly preceded him in 1982–83. "**Johnny O'Neal** was one of the most interesting guys to fill that seat. As a raw talent, he might be The One. Talk about natural talent. Art really, really loved Johnny because not only was he a natural player, he was a natural entertainer."

CHAPTER 5

THE BASS CLEF: TROMBONISTS & BASSISTS
The Big Beat

A HYPOTHETICAL:

You're a trombone player.

Your axe is inherently difficult to play. It requires you to use muscles that no other instrumentalist has to use: your deltoids, your triceps, your trapezius. You don't have any valves or keys to work with, only a slide, so intonation is always an issue. And while you can elicit a bevy of loud noises from your 'bone, laying down smooth solo lines at a brisk hard-bopping tempo requires a higher-than-high level of proficiency.

Now ask yourself: How do you stand your ground when your band-leader is a tornado?

Do you "dumb down" your improvisations, i.e., play slower and more minimalistically? Do you kick out some harmonically complex lines in order to compensate for any hindrances? Or do you put your head down, slide like you've never slid before, and try to out-tornado the tornado?

Another hypothetical:

You're a bass player.

Your axe is inherently difficult to play. It requires you to use muscles that no other instrumentalist has to use: your distal phalanges, your lumbricals, your adductors. You don't have any valves or keys to work with, only an unmarked fretboard, so intonation is always an issue. And while you can elicit a bevy of loud noises from your upright, laying down smooth walking lines at a fast tempo requires a higher-than-high level of proficiency.

Now ask yourself: How do you stand your ground when your rhythm section partner is a tornado?

Do you latch onto the cyclone's hi-hat and hold on for dear life? Do you position your notes one or two milliseconds behind the beat in an attempt to keep the whole group from flying off the stage? Or do you put your head down, pluck like you've never plucked before, and try to out-tornado the tornado?

These are the types of questions that had to be answered on a nightly basis by all Jazz Messengers trombonists and bassists.

Thanks to both the Messengers persona—fast, loud, complex—and Art Blakey's powerhouse drumming, being one of Buhaina's bass cleffers could be a pain in the arse. The trombonists, of which there were very few for understandable reasons, didn't just have to worry about keeping their head above water, they had to deliver improvs on the level of frontline cohorts like Wayne Shorter, Freddie Hubbard, and Javon Jackson. And the bassists had to generate an imaginative rhythm section foundation while subverting their more lavish ideas so as not to overshadow the chief Messenger.

Few listeners would deny that the Messengers 'bonists and bassists had it rough. But none would deny that Curtis Fuller, Jymie Merritt, Charles Fambrough, and Robin Eubanks were more than up to the task of staying on top of the bottom.

SOULNIK
Doug Watkins

"Doug Watkins set the table for all the Messenger bassists."
—Charles Fambrough

IF ART BLAKEY hadn't become a drummer/bandleader/jazz icon, he might well have made an excellent public address announcer. Just dig this player intro from the first volume of *The Jazz Messengers at the Café Bohemia*:

"On the bass … all the way from Motor City … ladies and gentlemen … one of the youngest and finest bass players in the business today … our bass player … Doug … *Wat*kins."

With that ringing overture, you'd expect that the aforementioned Motor City bassist would have the ability to hold down a hard bop bottom lower than a hard bop bottom had ever been held down before. You'd expect that his extended improvisations would flow, float, and fascinate. You'd expect that he would not only complement, but also enhance, Buhaina's bashing.

Your expectations would be met.

"Doug Watkins was a *great* bass player," bassist Lonnie Plaxico said. "His playing was *correct*."

A phenomenal musician in his own right, Watkins had another claim to fame in that he was brother-in-law to one of his era's most renowned bassists, a fellow Detroiter named Paul Chambers. Considering their familial and geographical proximity, it was little surprise that Watkins's style was not too distantly related to that of his not-too-distant relative. "Doug Watkins was coming out of the Paul Chambers school," Charles Fambrough said. "He liked to do all those double-stops like P.C." Throughout his 1954–56 Messengers run, Watkins would flash his Paul-ness all through his rare solo opportunities, as witnessed on his ballad feature, "What's New" (*Café Bohemia, Volume 1*). He kicks off the tune with a sweet rendition of the melody, which he follows with a chorus of low-register improv laden with double-stopped and double-timed runs straight out of his bro-in-law's bag o' tricks. (That solo by the first Messengers stringman was the kind that caught the ear of the last Messengers stringman: "Doug Watkins was sort of an extension of Paul Chambers," Essiet Essiet said, "and I was *really* into Chambers when I was growing up—which meant I was also really into Doug.")

Sound-wise, Watkins's full, fat timbre was consistent with the times. Admittedly, it's somewhat difficult to determine his true sonority, partly because in the mid-'50s, the recording techniques used by Blue Note engineer Rudy Van Gelder tended to make bassists on most Blue Note recordings sound relatively similar in tone. But his woody resonance compared favorably to that of Chambers and the rest of his contemporaries; since this rotund type of sound was more or less the standard of the era, Doug could be viewed as a model hard bop walker. On the up-up-up-tempo renditions of "The Theme" and "Minor's Holiday" from *Café Bohemia, Volume 1*, his quarter-note walking lines—virtually eighth-note- and triplet-free—are elegant in their simplicity; it's almost as if his right hand and Blakey's hi-hat were fused as one. But that's not to say that Watkins couldn't hop and skip when the situation called for hopping and skipping. His buoyant accompaniment on the greasy take of Benny Goodman's blues "Soft Winds" is full of well-timed hitches and hiccups, particularly during Hank Mobley's amicable solo.

Sadly, Watkins was only twenty-eight years old when he was killed in a car accident. Although he recorded with John Coltrane, Sonny Rollins, and Charles Mingus, it was Doug's work with the Jazz Messengers that encapsulated his voice, his concept, and his burgeoning individuality. Though minimal, his recorded output was a great inspiration to future Messengers bassists. "It's tragic that Doug Watkins didn't get a chance to really develop," Plaxico lamented. "Just tragic."

MERRITT OF DISTINCTION
Jymie Merritt

"Jymie Merritt was made for Art Blakey."

—Lonnie Plaxico

SOME BUHAINA-PHILES feel that Cedar Walton is the ultimate Jazz Messengers pianist, while others would bequeath that crown to Bobby Timmons. A goodly percentage would cite Lee Morgan as the supreme Jazz Messengers trumpeter, but Freddie Hubbard would unquestionably garner more than a handful votes.

But when it comes to the bass chair, there's zero question in anybody's mind that Jymie Merritt was The Man.

"Jymie Merritt is one of the greatest bassists in the history of the music," Charles Fambrough said. "What he did with the Messengers was incredible." Exemplified by a ceaseless groove, flawless timekeeping, and an uncanny ability to simultaneously play off of both his rhythm section and his front line, Merritt's many-leveled, "incredible" conception is the principal reason he holds the world record for Most Recorded Appearances with Art Blakey and the Jazz Messengers, Sideman Division.

Yet *another* one of those ubiquitous Philly-born Messenger phenomena, Merritt, while classically trained, spent his formative years plucking electric bass with R&B and soul types like B. B. King and Bull Moose Jackson. Lonnie Plaxico believed it was Jymie's hands-on blues experience that instilled him with The Groove. "Jymie Merritt was historically overlooked in the sense that out of the old jazz cats, he already had a funk thing going on. He's not a Paul Chambers type of player who was deep inside of the chord changes, but his approach stuck out just as well as P.C.'s."

During Jymie's 1958–62 tenure with the Messengers, the band underwent three major face-lifts: Merritt first backed the Lee Morgan/Benny Golson partnership, then the Lee Morgan/Wayne Shorter duo, then finally Freddie Hubbard/Wayne Shorter/Curtis Fuller triumvirate. All three of those front lines—while irrefutably Messenger-ish—were fundamentally varied in their respective approaches, but Jymie assimilated himself into each group, demonstrating that his most remarkable attribute was his ability to match his style with that of his bandmates.

The most perceptibly funky Messenger since Horace Silver, Merritt—more so than any Blakey bassist before or since—immediately made a major impact on the band. Throughout the in-concert smoker *Paris 1958* (BMG/Bluebird), his unyielding support creates a lush backdrop for the band's primary soloists, regardless of the tune's tempo or volume. Benny Golson's "Out of the Past"—a charming mid-tempo ballad in the vein of "Whisper Not"—is the kind of song that requires the bassist to provide both a sense of delicacy, so as not to break the tender mood, and a sense of propulsiveness, so as not to extinguish the forward thrust. Conversely, on the jaunty rendition of Charlie Parker's blues "Now's the Time," his austere quarter-note lines seem to be as much of an inspiration to the soloists as Blakey's loquacious accompaniment.

Merritt made his first perceptible stylistic leap when Shorter joined the band the following year, diversifying both his rhythmic and harmonic line of attack. On the live rendering of Morgan's brisk chameleonic blues "The Midget" (*Live in Stockholm 1959*, Dragon), he's more commanding and confident than he was the previous year—glissandos, forays into the upper registers, and inventive note choices rule the day. Plus, he took a bull-in-a-china-shop attitude toward the music, refusing to take any musical guff from Buhaina.

In 1961, when Hubbard replaced Morgan and Fuller was brought into the fold, not only did Jymie not miss a beat, but his playing became even more complex, more empathic, and more poised. Merritt was the ideal foil all through the album simply titled *Art Blakey and the Jazz Messengers* (Impulse, 1961), jamming and slamming over each of the different feels and vibes. Morgan threw down the melody on the knotty arrangement of the standard "Invitation," but rather than keep time, Jymie was obliged to play a unison background riff alongside Shorter and Fuller; that riff was a toughie—obviously written by a horn player, for a horn player—but the bassist jumps all over his fretboard with apparent effortlessness, not only nailing the line, but virtually carrying the song.

Mere months after the Impulse session, Merritt made another quantum musical leap, as illustrated on "Backstage Sally" (*Buhaina's Delight*). In this Shorter-composed shuffle sustained by an alternately ascending and descending chromatic chord structure, Jymie simply eats up the tortuous changes, loading his state-of-the-art lines with his now-trademark triplets. "The rhythms that he plays on 'Backstage Sally,'" Plaxico said, "that's something that could work in R&B."

Like the majority of the Messenger bottom-keepers, Merritt wasn't allotted a huge amount of solo space; but also like the majority of the Messenger bottom-keepers, he shone when he was given the opportunity to step out front. His one chorus on the 1959 take of "Moanin'" (*Moanin'*) is a melodic mid-register dazzler, a model of restraint and musicality. Three years later, his "Moanin'" solo allotment was doubled to two choruses (*A Day With Art Blakey*, IMC Records, 1961); correspondingly, also doubled were the quality, the volume, and the melodicism of his improvs.

Awesome accompaniment and stellar soloing aside, Merritt stuck with the Jazz Messengers for so long primarily because of the gluelike communication between himself and Buhaina. "The hookup Jymie Merritt had with Art Blakey was matchless," Plaxico said. "But Jymie was strong enough to stand alone. Sometimes, when I listen to those Jazz Messenger recordings, he's the only musician I can hear."

FULLER LOVE
Curtis Fuller

"Curtis Fuller made me realize that a trombone could play this style of music."

—Robin Eubanks

BRIAN LYNCH may have never touched a trombone in his life, but when it comes to discussing sliders and their place in the jazz pantheon, the trumpeter knows of what he speaks: "If anybody wants to look at a real jazz musician, they should look at Curtis Fuller. Curtis was someone who was very important to me on both a musical and personal level. I love his conciseness of expression. He's a *real* one."

Lynch's bandmate Steve Davis also recognized Fuller's station in hard bop history. "Curtis Fuller is, without a doubt, one of the biggest influences ever in the long legacy of improvising trombonists. Very few, if any, have played trombone on as many important recordings with as many influential bands in the history of jazz music. Perhaps none of those recordings are more important than the extensive body of classic recordings Curtis made with Art Blakey and the Jazz Messengers during the early and mid-1960s."

By the time he joined Bu's crew in 1961, the Detroit-born Fuller was already well known by both casual and hard-core jazzers alike; he had a dozen solo albums under his belt, plus he'd recorded and/or performed with saxophonists Benny Golson, Cannonball Adderley, and Yusef Lateef, as well as guitarist Kenny Burrell. His stout 'bone tone, his accessible solo lines, and his individualistic hop-skip eighth-note attack were well established, thus it was likely that the Messengers' musical director at the time, Wayne Shorter, gleaned that Curtis would be an ideal complement to both his own cerebral philosophy and Freddie Hubbard's brashness.

It was fortunate for all concerned that the trombonist was an experienced studio maven, as the Messengers cut a trio of albums over Curtis's first nine months with the group. *Mosaic, Buhaina's Delight*, and *Art Blakey and the Jazz Messengers* were waxed in bang-bang-bang fashion; considering this was the first time Blakey had ever expanded his band into a full-time sextet, it was impressive that the trio of recordings came across as if this edition had been together for years—thanks in no small part to Mr. Fuller. Curtis's four choruses on Shorter's mid-tempo minor-key "Reincarnation Blues" from the second session are a microcosm of his conception, filled with easy eighth-note runs, technically staggering triplets, and sunny euphonies. And while the presence of another instrument would obviously bulk up the ensemble, Fuller's distinct fatness bulked things up to a point that future Messenger ensembles could only aspire to.

His improvs were superlative, but his pen was also valuable to the group, as substantiated by the fact that two of his compositions became permanent fixtures not just in the Jazz Messengers repertoire, but also in the hard bop canon. A semi-exotic, semi–Middle Eastern, wholly charming mid-tempo swinger, "Arabia" is ideal for the three-man front line—Hubbard, in particular, has a blast getting busy over the conducive-to-getting-busy chord changes—plus the song fits hand in glove with the rest of the *Mosaic* session. And "A La Mode" from the Impulse date is, as one would guess, a modal-ish, bluesy jam whose just-above-medium-and-just-below-fast tempo and cheery, uplifting vibe are meat and potatoes not just for Fuller and his fellow horns, but for Blakey himself.

A kindly soul, Fuller played well with others in all senses of the phrase, always eager to please, always open to suggestions. "Curtis and I ended up being very close," Cedar Walton said. "He would say that he liked me because I used to correct him and tell him not to exaggerate. Musically, I'd say, 'Curtis, that's not the kind of song you'd want to solo on.' I was sort of like his mentor, but not exactly. I was just a colleague who was trying to make sure he got his stuff right, because he didn't have the keyboard skill that the other members had in order to help him compose. But he knew what he wanted, and I was able to help him in some instances—but not *every* instance. That brought us together."

Steve Davis unabashedly worshiped Fuller, and was always ready and willing to extol his many virtues. "There was a period between 1994 and '95 when Curtis's health wasn't so good and he couldn't play for about fourteen months," Davis said. "I drove up for many visits during that time, just to be there and talk, maybe listen to some music and hang with the family. I learned so much during those visits—sure, we discussed trombone stuff and may have gotten the horns out once or twice for about five minutes. But, honestly, our conversations have never really been about all that. I think that the main thing

I've learned, and am still learning, from Curtis is how important the feeling of this music and knowing its history really is.

"Curtis is certainly a hero and inspiration to me," Davis continued. "He always talked about Buhaina and how he loved playing in the Messengers with Freddie Hubbard, Cedar Walton, and Wayne Shorter. I consider myself very fortunate to know him, to have learned from him and played next to him—and most of all, to call him a friend. He set such a standard for the trombone chair—it's Curtis's footprints, and you're in them. On all those recordings, the Messengers' sound was so special, and bringing Curtis into it just filled it out. He's like a warm blanket under the sound, but he could step out and play the lead when he needed to. His ensemble sense is really impeccable. He's a masterful technician, and totally melodic and swinging. He made it possible for the rest of us to say, 'Wow. Curtis was cookin' in that band. Maybe we can do that too.' He had all that fire, and all that finesse—it was really something to behold. Curtis embodies what it is to be a Messenger in every way."

ALTERED SPACES
Reggie Workman

> *"Reggie Workman was very individualistic. Which is cool—I tend to want to hear what a guy has to say on his own rather than following the traditional thing."*
>
> —Lonnie Plaxico

THE BOTTOM keepers who plucked their way into and out of the Jazz Messengers were, for the most part, young, impressionable, and oftentimes malleable, so it generally wasn't too much of a problem for Buhaina (or whoever the Messengers' musical director happened to be at the time) to mold the bassist's style so he would suit the group's criteria. Reginald Workman, on the other hand, entered the band with an established musical persona, the only stringman to have joined and left the Jazz Messengers without being entirely Blakey-ized.

Before connecting with Blakey in 1962, Workman—yes, *another* Philly-born Messenger—had made his bones as a member of John Coltrane's quartet. His free-flowing concept was the perfect fit for Trane's band; performing alongside the elastic rhythm team of McCoy Tyner and Elvin Jones, Workman was the embodiment of unrestraint and abandon, always hovering over and under both the pulse and the chord structure. "Reggie worked so well with Trane because he's more free and experimental," Lonnie Plaxico said.

But in 1962, the Messengers sound was hardly free; while the band had stuck a tentative toe into the post–hard bop waters, the band's sense of group discipline was more or less the antithesis of the Coltrane quartet's individualistic autonomy—not better, not worse, just different. So how did the marriage between the insurgent Workman and the traditionalist Blakey survive?

Simply said, the union worked because Reggie Workman was a damn good bass player who could wedge himself into any setting without sacrificing his individualism. Still, he was coming off of a ride on the Coltrane, and the tenorist's concept was so potent that Workman wasn't able to wholly shed his Trane uniform. So in spite of the fact that Workman was an assimilator nonparell, the Messengers rhythm section adapted to Reggie more than Reggie adapted to the rhythm section, a factor that made for some interesting give-and-take. On the vamp-based "Nihon Bash" (*Kyoto*), Blakey and Cedar Walton lay down the mandated dotted-quarter-note-eighth-note groove—a groove that Reggie all but ignores; instead, the bassist meanders around the pulse, creating a gruff tension that never wanes.

But Reggie's insurgence is most evident throughout all four cuts on *Free for All*. "Reggie was still doing the Trane thing," Charles Fambrough said. "He played hard, but he played a lot of stuff in the upper register." On "Hammer Head," a jittery Wayne Shorter–penned shuffle, Workman works as if he's plucking next to Elvin Jones rather than Art Blakey. Instead of walking straight through the tune, he messes with the rhythms big-time, slithering behind and ahead of the beat; instead of keeping the bottom down, he spends much of the song touching base (or bass) in the mid-to-high registers. There are glissandos, there are double-stops, there are growls, and, most noticeably, there's a sense of authority and dominance never heard before or after from a Messengers bassist. Truth be told, Reggie Workman might have been the only bassist to out-Blakey Blakey, if only for the briefest of moments.

Though he never strayed far from his against-the-grain, cutting-edge timekeeping, Reggie Workman demonstrated that if you had the conviction, the feel, the chops, and the work ethic, you could make a significant mark on the Messengers. "Reggie was really good in the support role, supporting all kinds of different players who played in all kinds of different styles," Essiet Essiet said. "If you were a bass player with Art, you had to be a workhorse—and Workman was *definitely* a workhorse."

'BROSKI
Charles Fambrough

"Charles Fambrough was loose, relaxed, and playful. He brought a different kind of vibe into the band."

—James Williams

THIS ANECDOTE courtesy of Branford Marsalis kind of sums up what Charles Fambrough is all about:

"Sometimes when I'd be soloing, and Fambrough would be playing with the bow, he'd goose me in the ass with his bow when I'd hit a certain note. One time I was playing a ballad, and I was holding a note, and my eyes were closed. That whole time, Fambrough was positioning his bass so he could get my ass with the bow while I was hitting the last note. I nearly leapt out of my skin."

Yet *another* Philly phenom, Fambrough had a charmingly mischievous attitude and forceful bass attack that helped make the Messengers rhythm section of the early 1980s a happy place to be.

The bassist established himself doing sideman work with saxophonist Grover Washington, Jr., percussionist Airto, and pianist McCoy Tyner before joining Blakey—whom he met while bopping around the international jazz circuit—in 1980. "When I was playing with McCoy, we used to do a lot of festivals and double bills with the Messengers," Fambrough explained. Charles's distinctly Philly-based style (think Jymie Merritt filtered through future Messenger/fellow Philadelphian Stanley Clarke) fit perfectly next to Blakey and the steadfast James Williams; plus Fambrough's musical virility helped seal the bond between the Wynton Marsalis/Bobby Watson/Billy Pierce front line and the rhythm section.

When he wasn't goosing asses or sealing bonds, Fambrough was single-handedly catapulting the Jazz Messengers' acoustic bass tone into the electric era. "Charles came into the band right around the period that the direct box became standard," Lonnie Plaxico explained. "The whole sound of the upright bass changed. It changed the sound of the band, too—it was no longer the traditional Messengers sound. Charles's approach involved a lot of long tones; it was less traditional." (Fambrough's reason for plugging in to the direct box was pragmatic: "I wanted to make sure that each and every note that I played was heard.")

Sure enough, Fambrough's every note was heard right from jump street. On the live rundown of "Free for All" from *Art Blakey Is Jazz*, he plays the vamp exactly as it was written by Mr. Shorter—unlike Reggie Workman on the original recording—and his commanding, electric sound gives the song some added bounce and pliancy.

When it came to selecting notes, complementing his bandmates, and cranking out melodic solos, Fambrough was aces; this profusion of positive qualities is made plain on the leadoff cut from *Album of the Year*, "Cheryl." Exquisite in its brevity, the Charlie Parker blues may have been intended as a showcase for Wynton Marsalis and Bobby Watson, but in the end, it was Broski's just-in-front-of-the-beat lines that tied the whole thang together. As a reward for his superb accompaniment, Fambrough was given a solo (he trades four-bar phrases with the front-liners); he takes full advantage of his moment in the spotlight, laying down what, at that point, was possibly the most technically proficient solo ever waxed by a Messengers bassist.

Fambrough was a strong player coming into the band, but having Buhaina on his tail night in and night out bulked him up exponentially. All through *Keystone 3*, his final recording with the Messengers, Charles is a loose cannon, his churning lines urging Billy Pierce and both Marsalises to pump up their volume.

One of the few compositional contributions to the Messengers by a bassist, Fambrough's "Little Man" is a style-shifting, mid-tempo jewel that became a permanent fixture in the Blakey songbook. "On 'Little Man,' he was able to fit more of his own personality into the tune," Plaxico said, "and that also kind of changed the band's sound. And it's not necessarily a Philly thing—he's Afro-American, and that's just his language."

The connection between the bassist and Buhaina was deep on both a musical and personal level. "Art trusted me," Fambrough said. "Some gigs, at the end of the night, he would give me an envelope filled with our pay—sometimes it would be $30,000. He knew I'd just give it back to him in the morning." Blakey loved Fambrough so much that when the bassist brought in an original blues tune, Buhaina insisted it be called "Broski." "I would never name a tune after myself. But it was an honor—how many people can say that Art Blakey named one of their tunes?" (The Messengers never recorded the tune, but Fambrough included it on his first solo album.)

Unlike almost every other Messenger, Fambrough was one sideman Blakey refused to toss from the nest. "After three years, I left to do my own thing, even though Art told me, 'You're not ready to go. You need one more year.' Now I regret that I left."

Charles may have wished he'd hung on a bit longer, but during his tenure, he earned the respect of stringmen throughout the jazz world. "Fambrough is a strong player, very creative," Essiet Essiet said. "I have a lot of admiration for him." As did pretty much everybody else—even those who got goosed in the ass.

MELANGE
Lonnie Plaxico

"Lonnie Plaxico was always grooving."

—Charles Fambrough

IT'S SAFE to say that Lonnie Plaxico is the only musician in Jazz Messengers history whose primary influence is a member of the legendary soul/R&B/funk ensemble Earth, Wind & Fire.

"When I was with the Messengers, I played [EW&F bassist] Verdine White bass lines whenever I could," the Chicago-born Plaxico said. "Whenever we played [the Walter Davis Jr. composition] 'Jodi,' I tried to use the slides and the attack that Verdine liked to use; I tried to put more of the funk into the music."

On the surface, the pulsating walking lines Plaxico plucked while situated adjacent to Art Blakey don't have much in common with Verdine's galumphing funky grooves. But that's only on the surface—step down one level, and you'll comprehend that Lonnie's bass lines, while as hard bopping as they wanna be, aren't the kind of one-two-three-four-with-grace-notes-and-accents kind of bass lines generally associated with the Jazz Messengers, let alone straight-ahead jazz. But even though his concept diverged from the Messengers norm, he was nonetheless beloved by the brotherhood of Blakey bassists. "Lonnie was sort of a perfect player," Essiet Essiet said. "He plays like he has perfect pitch—he could hear what other people were playing and complement it perfectly. He never played out-of-tune notes, or 'wrong' notes."

Considering the scope of his methodology, Plaxico's somewhat traditional contempo-bop background—as well as his path to the Messengers—is a bit incongruous. "Terence Blanchard and Donald Harrison had a lot to do with me getting into the Messengers," he said. "I was twenty-two years old and playing with Dexter Gordon when I met [Blanchard and Harrison] in Morocco. Not too long after that, I did a week with Terence and Woody Shaw at the Blue Note; one day, not long after that gig, I was at home, and I got a phone call, and there was this funny voice on the phone that said, 'This is Art Blakey.' He asked if I wanted to play with the band. I wasn't even trying to get that gig—it's one of those gigs you just *wished* you had. I also thought that Charles

Fambrough was doing a good job with the band, and I figured that they didn't need me. But Art Blakey was always looking for younger musicians, and Fambrough had subbed out, and if [the current player] subbed out, he sometimes didn't get back into the band. I got lucky." Lonnie's Messengers entrée was eased in part by the fact that he had home court advantage for his initial performance. "My first gig was at the Jazz Showcase in Chicago. After that, I hit the road with him, and the rest is history."

From note one, Plaxico was compelled to set a new standard for Messengers bassists, in part because his background dictated that he *had* to. "I'd been playing professionally since I was 14, and I started out playing electric bass in R&B bands around Chicago. My style, when I joined the band, wasn't established yet, but the frame of mind I had was to not be a follower— I didn't want to play like other bass players. When I first started playing with Blakey, I'd given up trying to sound like Paul Chambers or Ray Brown. I would learn from them, but I wouldn't try and copy."

He may not have aped either Chambers or Brown, but on *Blue Night*— his first studio recording as a Messenger—Plaxico sounds as if he'd paid a whole bunch of attention to his direct predecessor: Like Charles Fambrough, Plaxico jumps the beat to fine effect; his walking on the Jean Toussaint–penned title cut provides a tension to the minor-keyed blues waltz, a song that, minus Lonnie's strong bass, might have lapsed into ordinariness. Like Fambrough, Plaxico possessed a round, punchy tone that slashed through Blakey's barrage; on the alternate version of Harrison's "Mr. Combinated"—a rendering much more frenzied than the master take— Lonnie's rotund sound helps goad Blanchard into a wildly exciting, almost out-of-control solo. And finally, also like Fambrough, Plaxico contributed an original composition that ultimately became a part of the Messengers repertoire, the record's evocative, über-melodic mid-tempo title cut.

But Plax's funky grooves were most evident on the band's live recordings. If you isolate his lines on the sped-up take of "On the Ginza" (*Live at Ronnie Scott's, London*, Hendring/Wadham, 1985), you'll catch the kinds of syncopated, staccato eighth notes associated with contemporary rhythm and blues. Though riveting in its newness, it was this sort of unique approach to accompaniment that augured the end of Plaxico's days as a Jazz Messenger. "Art allowed me to work on a lot of rhythmic things," Lonnie said. "By my last year with the Messengers, the kind of music I was working on probably wasn't suitable for the band. I was going back to playing more electric bass and getting back into some other styles of music. I wanted to not be labeled as strictly a jazz musician. They probably needed to get someone else." (From his perspective, Fambrough was impressed by Plaxico's insatiable urge to expand his vocabulary. "Lonnie was always trying to do stuff, always trying to change it up, and that was cool.")

Though at times Lonnie's musical concept clashed with Blakey's, the bassist always retained a more than healthy respect for his boss, if only because of the drummer's professional acumen and overall music biz savoir-faire. "The music industry is real political, and Art was not a political band-leader. But he was *real* cool. Being with the Messengers was one of the best experiences of my jazz career."

WAKEUP CALL
Robin Eubanks

"Don't mess with Robin. Don't even think about it."

—Steve Davis

ROBIN EUBANKS has 'tude.

It's not a bad kind of 'tude, not like the sort of 'tude associated with, say, a highly paid professional athlete who's been relegated to the bench. No, Robin's 'tude is a wholly positive one, stemming in some measure from the world's lack of understanding of his chosen instrument.

"When some people think of the trombone," Eubanks said, "they think of a big, cumbersome thing that has to play whole notes. When they think of trombone solos, they may take some sort of 'It's-okay-for-a-trombone' kind of attitude."

As evinced by his more than two mind-blowing years of work with the Jazz Messengers, the Philly-born Eubanks is the antithesis of the sloppy-whole-note-playing 'boner, a technician nonpareil. "When Robin was with the band, he was flyin' all over the horn," Steve Davis raved. "He was a great inspiration in that he exuded a lot of confidence in his playing. He gets an open, lyrical sound that's really hard to get. And technically? Forget about it."

Robin began listening to jazz as a teenager, but the burgeoning brassman was disappointed when he realized that mega-musical, technically proficient jazz trombonists were few and far between. So when he stumbled across his first Jazz Messengers album—an album that featured Curtis Fuller—he was justifiably psyched. "If nothing else, I just liked the fact that there was somebody on the record playing trombone."

Eubanks didn't necessarily set out to follow in Fuller's footsteps, but in 1980, he fell into a gig with the Messengers, touring that summer with Blakey's big band. His musical personality hadn't yet fully flowered, but the seeds of his full-fledged style had been planted and were raring to bloom. His brief improv on the Bobby Watson waltz "Wheel Within a Wheel" (*Live at Montreux and Northsea*) is both clever and convincing; he kicks off the solo with a neat quote from Charlie Parker's "Parker's Mood," and his flashy triplet runs and boisterousness take the tune to a higher plane. It should be noted that his was the song's second solo, preceding those of almost-grizzled veterans Watson and Billy Pierce; this possibly bespoke of Blakey's confidence in the youthful slidemeister.

By the time Robin took over the trombone chair in 1987, he was already an almost-grizzled veteran himself, having toured with Sun Ra and Stevie Wonder. His diverse experience and musical evolution is palpable; on the aforementioned 1980 live recording, Eubanks was right in the jazz tradition, his rhythmic attack and note selection straight out of the hard bop handbook, but by '87, he sounded like nobody other than himself. And while his innate inventiveness helped give his Messengers sextet its unique vibe, he still retained an affinity and veneration for his instrument's genesis in his chosen genre, as borne out by his playing on trombone legend J. J. Johnson's bop classic, "Kelo" (*Not Yet*). As with his "Wheel Within a Wheel" spot, Robin kicks off his solo with a quote—this one from "Chicago (That Toddlin' Town)"—before launching into two choruses replete with harmonically challenging squeaks and squawks. (Davis noted that Eubanks's palette is wider than those of many other trombonists, owing to a piece of 'bone-specific hardware. "He's one of the few guys who plays the horn with an F-extension, which is a sound that I like." Robin's explanation for his use of the add-on is a practical one: "An F-extension is like a low-C extension on an upright bass—it gives you a wider range.")

Robin's personal relationship with Blakey was similar to those of Bobby Watson and Javon Jackson in that the trombonist engaged in much offstage hanging out with the drummer; thanks to that quality time, the two developed a rapport that allowed for a certain amount of goofing around. Though Buhaina was an intensely spiritual man, he still teased Eubanks about his religious beliefs. "I'm a Buddhist, and Art used to make fun of me. I'd be sitting outside chanting, and he'd come up to me and ask, 'What're you doin', man? What's this all about?'" Filled with inner peace derived from his meditation, Eubanks easily laughed off his bandleader's gibes.

Blakey's fondness for Robin's on- and offstage personality was the primary reason he was chosen as the band's musical director, the only Messengers trombonist to hold that sacred position. But he eventually lost the job because he had the temerity to complain about his impending loss of hearing. "On stage, I was positioned by Art's ride cymbal, which was so loud that I'm still a little deaf in one of my ears. I asked Art if I could move to another part of the stage;

after that, he made Javon musical director."

Like Benny Green, Blakey gave Eubanks the opportunity to learn how to grab and hold a crowd all by his lonesome. "Art would rotate around the band and feature each person on a ballad—that was his break—so I learned how to pace my solos and how to play unaccompanied. You'd have to keep playing until he came back—it taught me to play by myself in front of an audience for a long time." And like dozens of Messengers before him, Robin was also trained by Blakey in the fine art of being a professional musician. "Art took me around the world and showed me the ropes. He was very instrumental in my development."

So to reiterate:

Robin Eubanks has 'tude.

It's not a bad kind of 'tude, not like the sort of 'tude associated with, say, a highly paid professional athlete who's been relegated to the bench. No, Robin's 'tude is a wholly positive one, stemming in some measure from the guidance of one Abdullah Ibn Buhaina.

VIBE UP
Steve Davis

"Steve Davis could represent."

—Robin Eubanks

IN HIS YOUNGER DAYS, Steve Davis was one emotional cat, which was why each and every day he spent with Art Blakey's Jazz Messengers was a roller coaster of feelings—especially those days he spent in the presence of various hard bop deities.

"I vividly remember the night we opened up at Catalina's in Los Angeles," the trombonist recalled. "Freddie Hubbard was there to listen, and I was scared to death; I was thrilled, and happy, and enjoying it … but I was also terrified." Blakey sensed his young sideman's thrall/happiness/enjoyment/terror, so immediately after the band took its leave of the dais, Buhaina donned his professorial robes. "After the first set, I was coming off the bandstand, and Art put his arm around me and said, 'Hey, Steve—during your solos, you make your statement, you build your solo to a climax, then you get the fuck out. Simple, right?' Once in a while he would tell you something like that to help you relax; he'd just break it down to the pure elements of music."

Upon joining the Messengers in 1989, Davis was more than ready to be taken under Blakey's wing, having already spent time under the tutelage of a notable former Messenger. "Jackie McLean, who was my teacher at Hartt School of Music, recommended me to Art, even though I'd never stood in the same room as the two of them. I was at home in Binghamton, New York, and I got a message from Professor McLean the day after Christmas—I was twenty-two years old and just out of college when I got that call. Jackie said, 'Get in touch with Buhaina right away. He's looking for you.'" So Davis called, and Blakey summoned the trombonist to the big city. "A friend drove me to New York immediately that afternoon so I could make the hit that night. I'd already planned to go into town to hear the Messengers that night—but just to listen, not to be in the band, so it was quite a thrill." In his excitement, Steve understandably slipped into space-out mode. "I wound up forgetting the keys to my apartment, so I had to wear someone else's suit. And there was no rehearsal, no music—I just had to show up at Sweet Basil and try to make it through the gig." (The group, at that point, had grown into a nonet, and the rostrum at Sweet Basil was tiny, so Davis, as the new kid on the Messengers block, was relegated to a less than ideal spot adjacent to the stage. "I was positioned way off on the side, with one foot on the bandstand.")

The eager trombonist was a sponge, eager to soak up any and all musical tidbits offered by Bu and his buddies. "Art had a way of planting seeds in his musicians that would grow for the rest of their lives," Steve said. "Talking to Jackie McLean, or Curtis Fuller, or Cedar Walton, they all say the same thing—Art had a way of playing that showed you what to play; he guided you [toward] what to play and what not to play without actually telling you verbally. He would develop your sense of structure, and set all the parameters, and that would go inside you."

Davis's development was immediate and impressive; only five months into his tenure, not only did he supply a composition that was eventually tabbed as the title cut of *One for All*, but his improvisational skills had also progressed enormously. On the aforementioned tune, he tailgates his way through two jaunty choruses, his eighth-note attack proudly Fuller-esque and his harmonic attack unpretentious and agreeable.

Early on, Steve was a tad wet behind the ears, but a few months of touring dried those ears right up. "It was a world of experience. I was really young, and on the road for the first time. When we went to Los Angeles and Seattle, that was my first trip anywhere off the East Coast. I learned a lot both on and off the bandstand." And while Blakey was his primary source of wisdom, Steve also gave his bandmates credit for doing some coaching of their own. "Javon Jackson and Brian Lynch were a big help; they kind of each took me under their wing in small ways. They told me what to look for in music, and, more importantly, what not to look for."

A modest soul, the trombonist believed that his contribution to the Messengers wasn't as critical as the Messengers' contribution to him. "Looking back, I don't think I was ready to be on that bandstand with all those great musicians—certainly with Art Blakey. I just played what I could. But that's how you learn."

BASS CLEF NOTES

THOUGH NOT as melodic as his predecessor Doug Watkins, **James "Spanky" DeBrest** was, in many ways, a throwback, a true blue-collar bassist who would have been as much at home in Count Basie's Orchestra, circa 1937, as he was in the Jazz Messengers, circa 1957. He never dropped the tempo, his harmonic work was steadfast, if a tad mundane, and he rarely, if ever, took a solo. To put it succinctly, Spanky did nothing more than what a hard bop bass player is supposed to do—he was the harmonic and rhythmic glue that held the rhythm section together.

Art Blakey and the Jazz Messengers with Thelonious Monk (Atlantic, 1958) is a prime example of Spanky's solidity. An uncharacteristically un-Messenger-like recording, the Monk set is rife with tension. Blakey and Monk had recorded and performed together many times previous to these 1957 sessions, but over the years, both had grown, evolved, and, to an extent, become set in their ways. Monk liked to leave a ton of space in between his beautifully bizarro piano solos.

All of which put Spanky in the unenviable position of playing traffic cop, a duty he handled with faultless aplomb. On the Thelonious-penned slow blues "Purple Shades," the pianist's two-chorus solo is a typical Monk masterpiece of dissonance; as Monk's lines skitter further and further away from the tonal center, DeBrest, bricklayer that he was, stays within the song's format, grounding the performance superlatively.

As Monk was a minimalist in terms of comping, it was Spanky's job to hold down the harmonic fort; in this instance, his propensity for root/five-based walking served the music well, especially on "Evidence," a labyrinth of a tune in which Monk pretty much sat on his hands during the solos.

Reggie Johnson was the lucky bassist whose task it was to rein in the stylistic mishmash of the Chuck Mangione/Keith Jarrett band. As it so happened, he acquitted himself quite well. On "Buttercorn Lady," his loping lines hark back to the Jymie Merritt era. "Recuerdo," another Mangione composition, is a 6/8 Afro-Cuban-tinged ballad, which includes what is probably Blakey's most minimalistic recorded performance; as Buhaina gently caresses his toms with mallets and Jarrett strums the strings inside the piano, Johnson—who is startlingly up-front in the mix—throws down a triplet-based ostinato that demonstrates impressive chops and solid intonation.

The 1968 live outing *Moanin'* (Laserlight) is a true sleeper, one of the more beguiling of the lesser-known Messengers recordings. Given the opportunity, the intriguing front line of tenor saxophonist Billy Harper, trombonist **Julian Priester**, and trumpeter Bill Hardman could have become as ambulant and gripping as the Shorter/Hubbard/Fuller crew. The band's bassist, **Larry Evans**, is a stirringly selfless player, imposing in his unobtrusiveness. As the horn players were particularly loquacious, and with Blakey in an exceptionally hyper mood, Evans's behind-the-beat bopping helps keep the Messengers train from derailing.

"Priester is a cat that is underacknowledged," Steve Davis said. "He's been in so many great bands, and on so many great record dates. He's a big inspiration to me. He has a special sound, a very expressive sound. That's number one with all of my favorite players. He knew harmony to a great degree. He had a knack to blend."

Child's Dance and *Mission Eternal* include some inspired bass work from another cat from the Philly fold, **Stanley Clarke**, as well as talented journeyman **Mickey Bass**. The leadoff cut on *Child's Dance*, Clarke's "Song for the Lonely Woman," is a Fender Rhodes–driven Latin number that could have been yanked off of Chick Corea's seminal fusion classic *Light As a Feather*. In a first for the Messengers, the two bassists perform simultaneously, Bass holding down the low end and Clarke twittering around up high. Toward the end of the tune, the two bassists launch into a duo improv spot, which Clarke dominates with his trademark thumb calisthenics.

Mickey was the band's touring bassist and held down the string duties for the remainder of the two sessions. *Mission Eternal* was an attempt to cross over into the land of fusion, which is reflected by Bass's evidently (and badly) amplified tone, a sound that, considering the Messengers' history of acousticity, is unexpected and jarring. That said, his predominantly low-register walking lines are rudimentary but effective, especially on the more Messenger-typical *Child's Dance* sessions. His support of returning-to-the-fold pianist Cedar Walton on the jaunty arrangement of "Without a Song" and Walton's "Fantasy in D" is warm and brawny, his innate ability to swing overcoming the thinness of his bass's tone.

Considering his lengthy Jazz Messengers tenure, Charles Fambrough knew what it took to be a Blakey bassist—and he knew that **Dennis Irwin** had *it*. "Dennis was the ultimate Messenger bassist," declared Fambrough. He knew the bassist's role in that band—to swing."

Lonnie Plaxico seconds that emotion. "Dennis's playing is straight up—nothing controversial. He knew the role of the bass."

Essiet Essiet *thirds* that emotion. "Dennis is a great musician. He knows so much about the traditional style, about the straight-ahead style of jazz. He also knows a lot about classical and Brazilian music, and I felt like his open-mindedness was impressive. Art was open to any style—you could always be yourself."

If anybody is qualified to discuss Irwin's position in the band, it's his partner in rhythm James Williams. "Dennis already had a nice hookup with Art, so it made it easier for me to lock in there. He had a good feeling. He was very helpful, because when I joined the band, there was practically no book in existence, so I had to lean on him so I could know what the changes were."

Donald Harrison has fond memories of his college buddy, trombonist **Tim Williams**. "Every night when we were at Berklee together, we'd have jam sessions organized by Tim. *Every* night."

In Steve Davis's mind, those sessions paid off big-time. "Tim always sounded great. I really enjoyed his playing." But it wasn't just his silky lines that stuck in Davis's head: "I remember that big gold tooth he had."

Though he was a California native, **Peter Washington**'s prime influences were a duo of Detroit bassmen.

"Peter was really into Paul Chambers," Essiet Essiet said. "That was his man. Peter hooked up with Blakey really well."

"Peter Washington's playing is excellent," Charles Fambrough said. "It goes back toward the Doug Watkins style of bass. Peter could swing. He was just like Dennis Irwin in that regard."

Indeed, like the Motor City dwellers, Washington was a four-on-the-floor pulse keeper who could swing like a pendulum—a quality that Buhaina was seeking after Lonnie Plaxico's freewheeling. "After Lonnie," Fambrough said, "I think Art wanted somebody who could just lay it down."

Plaxico concurred. "I had probably driven all the other musicians crazy by trying to take it in directions that might have made them uncomfortable. After me, Peter's playing might have been a relief to them. Not that I couldn't play traditional—I just didn't want to."

Perhaps the most tasteful of Buhaina's second-generation bass brigade, the baby-faced Washington became a Messenger in 1986 after an apprenticeship with saxophonist John Handy. His refined approach lends an almost courtly air to *Feeling Good*. At the time, the Messengers' four-man front line was well oiled and capable, but had a tendency to lose control—an ideal setting for Washington's obliging walking. Utilizing the entire fingerboard, he offers warm, supple support on the album's two Wayne Shorter tunes, "On the Ginza" and "One by One." His subtle swing is a seemly contrast to trumpeter Wallace Roney and altoist Kenny Garrett's agreeably raucous improvisations.

Leon Dorsey was to Peter Washington as Lonnie Plaxico was to Charles Fambrough—he made the musical transition from bassist to bassist as smooth as silk. In something of a full circle, the Messenger that Dorsey most resembles musically is Spanky DeBrest. As demonstrated on the up-tempo numbers "Yang" and "Mayreh" from *I Get a Kick Out of Bu*, his timekeeping is of the straight-up one-two-three-four variety, which, while not necessarily exciting, more than gets the job done.

There were so few trombone players in the Messengers that it's sort of shocking that in one of his final bands, Buhaina had two sliders in the front line: Steve Davis and **Ku-Umba Frank Lacy**. Though he's generally best known for his work with avant-garde folks like trumpeter Lester Bowie and multi-reedists David Murray and Oliver Lake, Lacy was a model Messenger. "The music of [Blakey's] era had a certain flow," Lacy said. "There are chord changes and a certain way to play. If you've studied the history of your horn, then it just flows and you'll feel free within that vibe."

Davis enjoyed the heck out of playing with Lacy. "I love Frank—he filled up the horn, and played very strong. He's just such a soulful player. It's all music with him. Every note counts. He's a very spiritual player. He has a very special sound. It's all heart and soul. He is a complete musician, but he happens to play trombone. He could pick up a brick or a rock or a piece of pipe and make music with it."

"Essiet Okun Essiet is the type of bassist who I would go out and buy a CD he was on, just to find out what he was doing," Lonnie Plaxico said. "He's a *phenomenal* player. He knows what's going on with traditional jazz. He works on different things, rhythmically and as a soloist. He has the right mindset for music—he's not set in one thing. He's open-minded. He's a doer."

Jazz Messenger–wise, Essiet was able to "do" because of what he "did" as a kid. "When I was growing up, I listened to a lot of jazz," the bassist said, "so I'd already heard a lot of Messengers records." Also helpful was his experience in performing with excellent percussionists. "I played with a lot of other great drummers before I joined the band, and that helped. It wasn't that hard for me to play with Blakey, because he just swung, and we were along for the ride. He just carried the whole band, all the time. Art used to say, 'You have to beat your foot. That way you can feel it.'"

Though in his thirties when he joined the band, Essiet still learned a thing or three from the master. "Art was very good at showing you how to handle yourself on or off the road. He instilled a real confidence [in you]. He knew how to go into a club [where we were playing], find the owner or manager, and ask for [how much money] he felt like we deserved. He'd say, 'If they don't give you what you deserve, you don't have to take it.' That was a real confidence builder. He showed you how to conduct yourself as a person, even outside of playing music — how to stand up for yourself, how to be more together."

But the two most important things Essiet Essiet took away from the Jazz Messengers were a sense of community and a sense of perpetuation. "The Messengers was like a big, huge family," he said. "People from the older editions would come around and sit in and hang out and just talk. There was a connection with everybody that played in the band, which was very cool. And when Blakey would start swingin', Javon Jackson and I would just look at each other, and it was like, 'Wow. This is incredible.' For me it was really special, because I'd listened to all these records before I'd joined the band. In a lot of ways, being in the Messengers was the high point of my musical life. It's too bad that there's nothing like that now, because it was such a great school."

THEORY OF ART
Messengers Pay Homage to Art Blakey

HORACE SILVER: Art Blakey swung twenty-four hours a day. He had energy, he had drive, and he put everything that he had into his music. He was an engine—that was just him. He gave a hundred percent of himself—even if he was sick, he gave everything he had on the bandstand. Whenever he played, he took care of business. He was never in a slump. He was always on top of it, swinging and cooking.

FREDDIE HUBBARD: Art Blakey gave us the incentive to play the music. He took us on the road, he gave us the uniforms. It was so beautiful, every time I think about it, I cry. Art Blakey made me a man.

JAMES WILLIAMS: Art was evangelistic in many ways. He wanted to have the music there for the people. He felt that music should be in the communities, not just in the concert halls and bourgeois jazz clubs. To him, it needed to be there where the people could feel it and get next to it.

TERENCE BLANCHARD: Art always had a fierce passion for the music. The thing that was great for me was that I got a chance to listen to him talk about all of my heroes. He'd tell me stories about them, which also made them very real people to me. He made them out to be very real people with extraordinary talent.

JAVON JACKSON: If Art Blakey hired you, he knew that you had the potential to be a leader. He had a knack of finding leaders. Even if you weren't a leader when you first joined the band, once you left, you had what it took to be a leader. He was able to inspire. It's not always easy for a band-leader to inspire people. He made you believe what we should all believe in life—that you should strive to be better than you are.

DONALD HARRISON: All the musicians who played with Art Blakey turned out great. I don't know why—he could just pick 'em. He taught us, "Don't quit, keep going, be a strong person, love the music." He'd say stuff like, "The audience sees you before they hear you." Art Blakey understood what was going on with the world, what was going on with the music. One of the greatest things about him that people don't realize is that he fine-tuned his lessons for each individual.

BOBBY WATSON: Art would put you in a shit-or-get-off-the-pot situa-tion—it was a trial by fire. He'd throw you out there, but he'd back you up and give you confidence, because he believed in you. He'd say, "You're with the Messengers—you don't have nothin' else to prove. Just *play*."

VALERY PONOMAREV: Blakey knew who belonged in his organization, whether it was a young guy, or somebody with a formal education, or some-body who hadn't played with other people. He just knew who should be his guy.

JOANNE BRACKEEN: How did Art Blakey pick 'em? I have no idea. He'd hear them once, and that would be it. He didn't ask anybody else's opinion, he just got who he wanted. And he was always right on.

DONALD BROWN: It was good to be around Art Blakey. He was a person who could spot talent. One of the things he'd say was most important aside from having talent was the work ethic. All the Messengers were always striv-ing to be better. Most people don't have the work ethic that it takes.

MULGREW MILLER: The sound of the band was shaped largely because Art Blakey was a big band drummer before he started up the Messengers. In his mind, I think he wanted it to be a small band that sounded like a big band.

BENNY GREEN: I was in awe of not just Art's drumming, but his sense of history. Even though I was too young to fully understand at the time, I could feel Chick Webb and Sid Catlett, I could feel that he'd played with Billy Eckstine's big band. Somehow he brought that all to the forum.

CHUCK MANGIONE: People think of Art's drumming as being loud and forceful all the time. But he was actually like a spaghetti sauce that your mother put on at 10 a.m. and just simmered all day. He could keep the fire and intensity going while just tiptoeing really lightly. Then, all of a sudden, one of those press rolls would come out of nowhere for a couple of bars before a downbeat, and you were off to the races. He played with more dynamics than any other drummer I've ever heard. He sometimes played so soft that the loud seemed louder. There are so many drummers that start loud and there ain't no place to go.

JAMES WILLIAMS: Art was arguably the greatest bandleader, certainly in small ensembles. But I would even go beyond that, because he touched so many musicians, as well as touching the people. He anointed the listeners with music, music that, as he said, would "wash away the dust of everyday life."

JAVON JACKSON: I don't take anything away from Duke Ellington, but considering the sacrifices that Art Blakey made for forty years, I think he's the most important bandleader in jazz history. Ellington basically kept the same band together, but Art always had a different group. Duke wrote for the sound of his personnel, but no matter what edition of the Messengers—be it the one with Chuck Mangione, or Freddie Hubbard, or Lee Morgan, or Donald Byrd, or Wynton Marsalis—it *always* sounded like the Messengers.

BENNY GREEN: If you put Art up on the bandstand with *any* group of musicians, that group is going to swing.

TERENCE BLANCHARD: When I was in the band, Art was always trying to get us to change the sound of the Messengers. He'd say, "Look, man, I want you guys to come up with some crazy stuff." We were playing at Sweet Basil's one time, and he said, "I want it to get to the point where we can just walk up on the bandstand and create a tune." People don't associate that kind of thinking with Art Blakey. I'm sitting there thinking, "Your personality is so strong that it's hard for us to break away from that sound." His best stuff was centered around his personality. I don't think he wanted us to stay in the envelope. He wanted to push things, but he was who he was.

VALERY PONOMAREV: Whoever played with the Messengers, they were not forced but lured into Art Blakey's music. Art Blakey played behind them and molded their playing. He brought the best out of them.

BENNY GREEN: Art was so ensemble-oriented that he would orchestrate your solo for you. He would give it dynamics, and shape, and form, and structure. In so doing, he would ultimately give you a sense of telling a story, of writing a letter. Because of that, when you left the band, you'd bring that sensibility to your playing and your writing. He breathed so much life into his players. I'm still very much continuing to benefit from my experience with Art.

WYNTON MARSALIS: All the former Messengers always acted like kids when they were around Art. He just was a true believer. The band was an institution because of him, and the energy he put into it. He was out there playing for no money, seeing to it that we could play. He taught everybody what the meaning of true belief was. Near the end, he couldn't hear, he was almost deaf—and he was still playing. Man, he was unbelievable. Phenomenal.

TERENCE BLANCHARD: Everybody who's played with that band, when they're around each other, they talk about Art. I don't care what the situation is; you could be in the middle of Camp David talking with the president, but if somebody else who was in the band shows up, you'll be like, *"D'you remember when Art...?"*

CHUCK MANGIONE: Musically, Art was very punctual. But with gigs, we were never really on time. One time we were scheduled to play in Philadelphia. We all pulled up in front of the club, and I saw a sign in the window that said, "Yusef Lateef." It turned out we were a month early for the gig. We still weren't on time.

BRANFORD MARSALIS: I was once talking with Art about Charlie Parker, and he said, "I remember when I played with Bird one time in this club. He came in, and one of the first songs he played was a ballad. He played ''Round Midnight.' And this is what he played..." He started singing the solo, and I'll be damned if it didn't sound exactly like Bird.

JOANNE BRACKEEN: Blakey hung out a lot. He'd go a couple of months without sleep, then he'd go home and sleep a *lot*.

CHUCK MANGIONE: Before Art would get on stage, he'd take four shots of Courvoisier, then chase it down with a Coke, then kind of shudder, then jump on the bandstand and say, "Here we go!" He was a fun-loving person who just brought everything to life.

BRANFORD MARSALIS: One time we were in Paris. The British ambassador to France was a big jazz fan, and at the end of the concert, he invited us over to his house for a party. He had thousands of jazz records, and one of the records featured Art when he was eighteen years old, playing with Cab Calloway. I said, "Let's put it on and see if he remembers it. Don't tell Art— just put it on and see if he remembers." Art was half drunk, for sure, and he was telling a joke when we put the record on. I walked over to the group he was standing with, and he continued to tell the joke, and the record's playing, and he gets to the joke's punch line, and everybody starts laughing, and he's laughing, and when he finishes laughing, he hears the record and says, "Hah. Boy, I'll tell ya, I was eighteen years old back then." Then he starts singing the song, singing the drum part, saying stuff like, "Boy, that Chu Berry was a bad muthafucka." He remembers every single hit from a gig that he hadn't played in over forty years. Some people think that all men are created equal— but most men couldn't recite a part that they'd played over forty years ago. All men are *not* created equal—Art Blakey was a very, very special man.

BRIAN LYNCH: The spirit of being a true Messenger is to bring a seriousness to it—and you're able to do it in a format that Art made. You can make your statements in an accessible format. The way he put it together, you could do all these serious, mindful things, but also get over and communicate to an audience and make it a viable proposition in terms of the entertainment business. That's one of the victories and triumphs of Art's style of music.

JOANNE BRACKEEN: Art Blakey was a master. He was incredible. After I left the band, I felt like I'd gone to Africa to study. Plus I really liked Art as a person. He used to call me his adopted daughter. Him and I thought the same way. I could never talk with my family the way I talked to him, because [my family] wouldn't know what I was talking about. We were on the same wavelength.

CEDAR WALTON: Art Blakey was the most intelligent person I'd ever met. Prior to meeting him, I'd equated intelligence with graduating from college and getting a master's degree. But I had it wrong—being around Art, you could see that intelligence was gained much faster by traveling, and performing, and being admired by people in high places.

STEVE DAVIS: It's truly a blessing and a privilege to say that I was a Jazz Messenger, and I'm still a Messenger. That was a dream come true for me to be on the bandstand with Art Blakey, and make a couple of records, and travel around. He was a true iron man.

BRANFORD MARSALIS: Art as a musician was nonpareil. That's what makes him different from other drummers, that he was a complete musician.

VALERY PONOMAREV: If you learn something from Art Blakey, you hold on to it. You cherish that for your whole life. He drew out of me what I didn't know I had.

BENNY GREEN: When you play with Art Blakey, you take a step toward the music—but the music also takes a step toward you.

JAVON JACKSON: He was a man's man. Think of the greatest man you know, and add about three hundred things on top of that, and you've got Art Blakey.

FREDDIE HUBBARD: They should put a statue of Art Blakey in Central Park.

THE SIDEMEN OF ART BLAKEY AND THE JAZZ MESSENGERS

"WHEN YOU LOOK at the guys in my generation, almost all of the guys played with the Messengers," Terence Blanchard said. "You go back to the generation before mine, and damn near everybody in that generation played in the band, with the exception of Herbie Hancock and a few other people." Indeed, while the sheer number of Hard Bop Academy scholars is in and of itself amazing, it's the quality of the sidemen that is truly mind-boggling.

Blakey-phile Michael Fitzgerald compiled a list of many, if not all, of the artists who sat or stood beside Art Blakey either on a dais or in a recording room. We've done our best to present a complete list; if we've missed anybody, please let us know, and we'll make corrections in future editions.

(An asterisk denotes either a short stint or a guest appearance.)

TRUMPET

Terence Blanchard (1982–86, 1987*, 1989*)

Randy Brecker (1968–9)

Bobby Bryant (1958*)

Donald Byrd (1955–56, 1981*)

Johnny Coles (1977*)

Olu Dara (1973–74)

Kenny Dorham (1954–55 1961*)

Jon Faddis (1983*, 1986*)

Frank Gordon (1976)

Colin Graham (1986*)

Bill Hardman (1956–58, 1961* 1967–68, 1970–71, 1973, 1975–76, 1979*, 1981, 1985*, 1987*)

Roy Hargrove (1988*)

Philip Harper (1987–88)

Eddie Henderson (1973–74, 1979*, 1980*)

Freddie Hubbard (1961–64, 1965*, 1976*, 1981*, 1982*, 1983*, 1984*, 1985*, 1988*, 1989*)

Brian Lynch (1988–1990)

Chuck Mangione (1965–66)

Wynton Marsalis (1980–82, 1983*, 1986*)

Lee Morgan (1957*, 1958–61, 1964–65)

Michael Philip Mossman (1987*, 1988*)

Shunzo Ono (1975*)

Jimmy Owens (1966*)

Valery Ponomarev (1977–1980, 1986*)

Wallace Roney (1976*, 1980–81, 1986–87)

Woody Shaw (1969, 1972–73, 1975*, 1983*, 1987*)

Don Sickler (1987*, 1988*)

Ira Sullivan *[also played tenor saxophone]* (1956)

Charles Tolliver (1965*)

SAXOPHONE

George Adams *[tenor]* (1972*)

Dale Barlow *[tenor]* (1989–90)

Gary Bartz *[alto]* (1965)

Ralph Bowen *[tenor]* (1987*, 1988*)

Don Byas *[tenor]* (1971*)

Charles Davis *[baritone]* (1964*)

Nathan Davis *[tenor]* (1965*)

Joe Farrell *[tenor]* (1968*)

Carlos Garnett *[tenor]* (1969–70)

Kenny Garrett *[alto]* (1986–87)

John Gilmore *[tenor]* (1964–65)

Benny Golson *[tenor]* (1958–59, 1979*, 1982*, 1983*, 1984*, 1985*, 1987*)

Johnny Griffin *[tenor]* (1957, 1981*, 1985*, 1986*)

Craig Handy *[tenor]* (1989*)

Billy Harper *[tenor]* (1967–68, 1979*, 1980*, 1981*)

Donald Harrison *[alto, soprano]* (1982–86, 1989)

Joe Henderson *[tenor]* (1967*)

Vincent Herring *[alto]* (1989*)

Marchel Ivery *[tenor]* (1982*)

Javon Jackson *[tenor]* (1986*, 1987–90)

Carter Jefferson *[tenor]* (1973–74)

Sonny Lewis *[tenor]* (1976*)

Jackie McLean *[alto]* (1956–57, 1979*, 1980*, 1981*)

Branford Marsalis *[alto]* (1980*, 1981–82)

Frank Mitchell *[tenor]* (1965–67)

Hank Mobley *[tenor]* (1954–56, 1959, 1975*)

Ramon Morris *[tenor]* (1971–72)

Cecil Payne *[baritone]* (1957*)

Billy Pierce *[tenor]* (1980–82, 1987*, 1989*)

Courtney Pine *[tenor]* (1986*)

Jerome Richardson *[baritone]* (1960*)

Nelson Santiago *[alto]* (1975*)

David Schnitter *[tenor]* (1975–80)

Sahib Shihab *[alto]* (1957*)

Wayne Shorter *[tenor]* (1959–64, 1966*)

James Spaulding *[alto]* (1964*, 1987*)

Buddy Terry [tenor, *soprano]* (1971*, 1972*)

Terence Tony *[alto]* (1989*)

Jean Toussaint *[tenor]* (1982–86)

Tyrone Washington [tenor] (1969*)

Bobby Watson [alto] (1977–81, 1986*, 1988*, 1989*)

Barney Wilen [tenor] (1959)

Steve Wilson [alto] (1988*)

Steve Williamson [tenor] (1986*)

TROMBONE

Steve Davis (1989–90)

Robin Eubanks (1980*, 1983*, 1987–89)

Curtis Fuller (1961–65, 1969*, 1973*, 1975*, 1977*, 1979, 1980–81, 1982*, 1983*, 1984*, 1985*, 1986*, 1989*)

Slide Hampton (1967, 1972*, 1976*, 1981*)

Frank Lacy (1988–89)

Melba Liston (1957*)

Julian Priester (1968, 1987*)

Steve Turre (1973*)

Tim Williams (1985–86)

PIANO

Kasal Allah (1975*)

Kenny Barron (1968*)

Joanne Brackeen (1970–72)

Donald Brown (1981–82, 1983*, 1986)

Jaki Byard (1965*)

George Cables (1969, 1972)

Chick Corea (1966)

Albert Dailey (1970*, 1975–76)

Walter Davis Jr. (1959–60, 1972*, 1975–77, 1981*, 1983*, 1984*, 1985*, 1986*, 1987*, 1989*)

Sam Dockery (1956–57)

Sonny Donaldson (1969*)

Russell Ferrante (1976*)

Benny Green (1986–89)

John Hicks (1964–65, 1972–73, 1976*)

John Houston (1958)

Keith Jarrett (1966)

Geoffrey Keezer (1989–90)

Wynton Kelly (1957*, 1968*)

Cedric Lawson (1974)

Harold Mabern (1975*)

Junior Mance (1957*)

Ronnie Matthews (1968, 1975*)

Mulgrew Miller (1983*, 1984–86, 1989*)

Amina Claudine Myers (1977)

Mike Nock (1966)

Johnny O'Neal (1982–83)

Don Pullen (1972*)

Horace Silver (1954–56)

Donald Smith (1971*)

Lonnie Liston Smith (1965–66)

Bobby Timmons (1958–61)

Mickey Tucker (1976)

McCoy Tyner (1966*, 1967*)

Cedar Walton (1961–64, 1973, 1979*, 1980*, 1981*, 1982*, 1985*)

James Williams (1977–81)

BASS

Chris Amberger (1976)
Jan Arnet (1969–70)
Mickey Bass (1970*, 1972*, 1973–74)
Juni Booth (1966–67)
Cameron Brown (1976, 1989*)
Stanley Clarke (1972)
Skip Crumby (1969*)
Spanky DeBrest (1956–58)
Hal Dodson (1971*)
Leon Dorsey (1988–89)
Essiet Essiet (1989–90)
Larry Evans (1968)
Charles Fambrough (1980–83)
Eddie Gomez (1965*)
Scotty Holt (1969*)
Dennis Irwin (1977–79, 1980*)
Stafford James (1973–74)
Reggie Johnson (1965–66)

Jymie Merritt (1958–62, 1975*, 1981*)
Charnett Moffett (1986*)
Lonnie Plaxico (1983–86)
Clarence Seay (1981*)
Avery Sharpe (1980)
Victor Sproles (1964–65, 1981*)
Isao Suzuki (1969*)
Yoshio Suzuki (1975–76)
Ben Tucker (1966*)
George Tucker (1958*)
Austin Wallace [electric bass] (1972*)
Wilbur Ware (1956*)
Peter Washington (1986–88)
Doug Watkins (1954–56)
Buster Williams (1968*, 1982*, 1983*, 1984*, 1989*)
Reggie Workman (1962–64, 1965*, 1975*, 1979*, 1985*, 1986*, 1987*)

OTHER INSTRUMENTS

Bill Barber [tuba] (1964*)
Nathaniel Bettis [percussion] (1972*)
Wellington Blakey [vocals] (1964)
Ladji Camara [percussion] (1976)
Buck Clarke [percussion] (1972*)
Kevin Eubanks [guitar] (1980*)
Pablo Landrum [percussion] (1972)
Tommy Lopez [percussion] (1959*)
Ray Mantilla [percussion] (1972–73, 1977*)
Sonny Morgan [percussion] (1972*)

Airto Moreira [percussion] (1979*, 1980*)
Essien Nkrumah [guitar] (1972*)
Emmanuel Rahim [percussion] (1972*)
John Rodriguez [percussion] (1959*)
Willie Rodriguez [percussion] (1959*)
Jeremy Steig [flute] (1972*)
Tony Waters [percussion] (1973*)
Julius Watkins [French horn] (1964*)

References

(Unless otherwise noted, all quotes are culled from interviews the author conducted August–October 2001.)

CHAPTER 1
ART BLAKEY: The Messenger and His Message

PRINTED SOURCES:
Art Blakey: "I used to play by ear…"
   —Ira Gitler, liner notes to *Like Someone in Love*, 1960
Art Blakey: "Horace Silver got Hank Mobley and
   Kenny Dorham and Doug Watkins and myself…"
   —*Cadence*, July 1981
Art Blakey: "It first started out being a cooperative thing…"
   —*ibid*
Art Blakey: "We didn't expect the band to go worldwide…"
   —*ibid*
Art Blakey: "I've had bands since I was fifteen years old…"
   —John Litweiler, *DownBeat*, March 25, 1976
Art Blakey: "He [Monk] was responsible for me…"
   —*ibid*
Art Blakey: "I lived in Boston during the war…"
   —Art Blakey, *Jazz Magazine*, winter 1979
Art Blakey: "The Jazz Messengers really started in 1949…"
   —Herb Nolan, *DownBeat*, November 1979
Art Blakey: "A couple of years later I went into…"
   —*ibid*
Art Blakey: "I'll play drums until Mother Nature tells me different…"
   —Brian Case, *Wire*, December 1984

Art Blakey: "I don't tell them what to play, I tell them what not to play…"
—*DownBeat*, Dec. 1988
Jackie McLean: "The school is closed for good."
—Mike Hennessey, liner notes to *The Art of Jazz: Live at Leverkusen*, 1989

OTHER SOURCES:
Art Blakey: "I like the Lee Morgan/Bobby Timmons/Benny Golson group…"
—recorded interview with Mike Hennessey, *The Art of Jazz: Live at Leverkusen*, 1976
Art Blakey: "When a guy gets so big, I have to fire him…"
— recorded interview with Alyn Shipton, *Jazz Legend*, 1985
Art Blakey: "I keep my foot in their behinds every night. I scare 'em to death."
—recorded interview with Alyn Shipton, *Jazz Legend*, 1985

CHAPTER 2
HIGH MODES: The Trumpeters

CONVERSATIONS: Freddie Hubbard, Brian Lynch, Chuck Mangione,
Branford Marsalis, Valery Ponomarev

KENNY DORHAM
CONVERSATIONS: Terence Blanchard, Freddie Hubbard, Brian Lynch,
Chuck Mangione, Wynton Marsalis, Horace Silver

DONALD BYRD
CONVERSATIONS: Brian Lynch, Chuck Mangione

BILL HARDMAN
CONVERSATIONS: Terence Blanchard, Joanne Brackeen, Freddie Hubbard,
Brian Lynch, Wynton Marsalis, Valery Ponomarev

LEE MORGAN
CONVERSATIONS: Terence Blanchard, Freddie Hubbard, Brian Lynch,
Chuck Mangione, Wynton Marsalis, Valery Ponomarev

PRINTED SOURCES:
Wayne Shorter: "Lee was different…"
Conrad Silvert, liner notes to *Africaine*, 1979
Lee Morgan: "I've always played a lot of notes…"
—Nat Hentoff, liner notes to *Search for the New Land*, 1964
Lee Morgan: "I don't think I have a completely original style…"
—*ibid*
"I don't like labels…"
—Michael Cuscuna, liner notes to *Tom Cat*, 1990

OTHER SOURCES:
Art Blakey: "Lee Morgan was always out there directing the music…"
    —Recorded interview with Mike Hennessey, *The Art of Jazz: Live at Leverkusen*, 1979
Art Blakey: "Bill Hardman was the one who went and got Lee Morgan…"
    —*ibid*

FREDDIE HUBBARD
CONVERSATIONS: Terence Blanchard, Donald Brown, Freddie Hubbard, Javon
    Jackson, Geoffrey Keezer, Brian Lynch, Wynton Marsalis, Valery Ponomarev

PRINTED SOURCES:
Art Blakey: "Freddie's so fantastic…"
    — *Jazz Magazine*, winter 1979

CHUCK MANGIONE
CONVERSATIONS: Chuck Mangione, Wynton Marsalis

WOODY SHAW
CONVERSATIONS: Terence Blanchard, Freddie Hubbard, Javon Jackson, Brian Lynch

VALERY PONOMAREV
CONVERSATIONS: Terence Blanchard, Brian Lynch, Wynton Marsalis,
    Valery Ponomarev

PRINTED SOURCES:
Valery Ponomarev: "About half a year…"
    —Larry Birnbaum, *DownBeat*, June 21, 1979

WYNTON MARSALIS
CONVERSATIONS: Terence Blanchard, Charles Fambrough, Freddie Hubbard,
    Brian Lynch, Chuck Mangione, Wynton Marsalis, Valery Ponomarev

PRINTED SOURCES:
Wynton Marsalis: "If I hadn't played with Art, I wouldn't have played jazz."
    —Mike Hennessey, liner notes to *The Art of Jazz: Live at Leverkusen*, 1989
Wynton Marsalis: "When I first sat in with him, I knew I wasn't playing nothing…"
    —Geoffrey C. Ward and Ken Burns, *Jazz: A History of America's Music*, Knopf,
    2000

TERENCE BLANCHARD
CONVERSATIONS: Terence Blanchard, Freddie Hubbard, Geoffrey Keezer, Brian
    Lynch, Wynton Marsalis, Valery Ponomarev

BRIAN LYNCH
CONVERSATIONS: Steve Davis, Brian Lynch

TRUMPET NOTES
CONVERSATIONS: Terence Blanchard, Freddie Hubbard, Valery Ponomarev

CHAPTER 3
NOISE IN THE ATTIC: The Saxophonists

CONVERSATIONS: Donald Harrison, Bobby Watson

HANK MOBLEY
CONVERSATIONS: Javon Jackson, Bobby Watson

JACKIE MCLEAN
CONVERSATIONS: Steve Davis, Javon Jackson, Bobby Watson

PRINTED SOURCES:
Jackie McLean: "I went with Art Blakey, the Daddy..."
   —Valerie Wilmer in *Jazz Journal*, July 1961

OTHER SOURCES:
Jackie McLean: "With Blakey, I had the most wonderful experience..."
   —Radio interview with Gary Walker, WBGO, 2001

BENNY GOLSON
CONVERSATIONS: Terence Blanchard, Javon Jackson, Geoffrey Keezer,
   Branford Marsalis, Valery Ponomarev, Bobby Watson

PRINTED SOURCES:
Benny Golson: "I said, 'Art, you're a great man...'"
   —Doug Ramsey, liner notes to *Paris 1958,* 1989
Benny Golson: "I went home that night to my room..."
   —*ibid*
Benny Golson: "In 1958, [the phone rang], and it was my hero..."
   —*ibid*
Benny Golson: "'What's all this Philadelphia stuff?...'
   —*ibid*
Benny Golson: "He was trying to tell me without words..."
   —*ibid*
Benny Golson: "Art Blakey was a teacher..."
   —Paula Edelstein, *AllAboutJazz.com*, Dec. 2000

OTHER SOURCES:
Benny Golson: "Alfred Lion at Blue Note..."
   —Radio interview with Gary Walker, WBGO, 2001
Art Blakey: "Benny Golson could always keep the band in line..."
   —Recorded interview with Mike Hennessey, *The Art of Jazz: Live at Leverkusen*,
   1989

WAYNE SHORTER

CONVERSATIONS: Terence Blanchard, Javon Jackson, Branford Marsalis, Bobby Watson

PRINTED SOURCES:
Wayne Shorter: "We were at a Canadian jazz festival…"
  —Conrad Silvert in *DownBeat*, July 1977
Wayne Shorter: "Art Blakey used my tunes right from the beginning…"
  —*ibid*
Wayne Shorter: "I went back and saw Art Blakey…"
  —Brian Case in *Wire*, December 1984
Wayne Shorter: "Miles called me…"
  —Mel Martin in *Saxophone*, January/February 1992

OTHER SOURCES:
Art Blakey: "We spent a lot of time—five or six years—bringing Wayne out of his shell…"
  —Recorded interview with Mike Hennessey, *The Art of Jazz: Live at Leverkusen*, 1989

DAVID SCHNITTER

CONVERSATIONS: David Schnitter, Bobby Watson

BOBBY WATSON

CONVERSATIONS: Donald Harrison, Branford Marsalis, Bobby Watson, James Williams

BILLY PIERCE

CONVERSATIONS: Javon Jackson, Billy Pierce

PRINTED SOURCES:
Billy Pierce: "I know what it takes to make me play…"
  —Billy Pierce, Saxophone Journal, Jan.-Feb. 1991

BRANFORD MARSALIS

CONVERSATIONS: Donald Harrison, Branford Marsalis, Bobby Watson

DONALD HARRISON

CONVERSATIONS: Donald Harrison, Javon Jackson, Branford Marsalis, Bobby Watson

JAVON JACKSON

CONVERSATIONS: Javon Jackson, Branford Marsalis, Bobby Watson

SAXOPHONE NOTES

CONVERSATIONS: Donald Harrison, Javon Jackson, Branford Marsalis, Bobby
　Watson

PRINTED SOURCES:
Kenny Garrett: "That was an institution, playing with Blakey…"
　—Fred Jung, *AllAboutJazz.com*, June 1999
Johnny Griffin: "My experience in Art's band was excellent…"
　—Len Lyons, *DownBeat*, August 1979

OTHER SOURCES:
Art Blakey: "It was a toss-up between John Coltrane and Wayne Shorter."
　—Recorded interview with Mike Hennessey, *The Art of Jazz: Live at Leverkusen*,
　1989

CHAPTER 4
ROOTS AND HERBS: The Pianists

CONVERSATIONS: Joanne Brackeen, Benny Green, Geoffrey Keezer, Horace Silver,
　James Williams

HORACE SILVER

CONVERSATIONS: Joanne Brackeen, Donald Brown, Benny Green, Geoffrey Keezer,
　Mulgrew Miller, Horace Silver, Cedar Walton, James Williams

PRINTED SOURCES:
Art Blakey: "Horace went out on his own and didn't look back…"
　—*Radio Free Jazz*, March 1977
Art Blakey: "It first started out being a cooperative thing…"
　—*Cadence*, July 1981
Horace Silver: "Art was a great guy and one hell of a drummer…"
　—Fred Jung, *AllAboutJazz.com*, September 1999

BOBBY TIMMONS

CONVERSATIONS: Donald Brown, Benny Green, Geoffrey Keezer, Mulgrew Miller,
　Horace Silver, Cedar Walton, James Williams

PRINTED SOURCES:
Bobby Timmons: "There is really no other group to go to from here…"
　—Leonard Feather, liner notes to *Meet You at the Jazz Corner of the World*, 1960
Bobby Timmons: "Soul is an innate thing in people…"
　Leonard Feather, liner notes to *Meet You at the Jazz Corner of the World*, 1960

OTHER SOURCES:
Benny Golson: "Actually, it was Bobby Timmons's tune…"
　—Radio interview with Gary Walker, WBGO

WALTER DAVIS, JR.

CONVERSATIONS: Joanne Brackeen, Donald Brown, Benny Green, Brian Lynch, Mulgrew Miller, Cedar Walton, James Williams

CEDAR WALTON

CONVERSATIONS: Joanne Brackeen, Donald Brown, Steve Davis, Benny Green, Mulgrew Miller, Horace Silver, Cedar Walton, James Williams

PRINTED SOURCES:
Cedar Walton: "The pianist, at least when I was with him…"
 —Arthur Moorhead, *DownBeat*, January 1981

KEITH JARRETT

CONVERSATIONS: Donald Brown, Chuck Mangione, Mulgrew Miller

PRINTED SOURCES:
Art Blakey: "It was really a misfit…"
 —*Cadence*, July 1981
Keith Jarrett: "It wasn't very easy for me to play with Blakey…"
 —Francois Postif, "Les Grandes Interviews de *Jazz Hot*," Editions de L'Instant, 1989

JAMES WILLIAMS

CONVERSATIONS: Joanne Brackeen, Donald Brown, Benny Green, Geoffrey Keezer, Mulgrew Miller, Horace Silver, Cedar Walton, James Williams

DONALD BROWN

CONVERSATIONS: Joanne Brackeen, Donald Brown, Branford Marsalis, Mulgrew Miller, James Williams

MULGREW MILLER

CONVERSATIONS: Joanne Brackeen, Donald Brown, Benny Green, Mulgrew Miller, Cedar Walton, James Williams

PRINTED SOURCES:
Mulgrew Miller: "With other groups…"
 —Gene Kalbacher, *DownBeat*, March 1988

BENNY GREEN

CONVERSATIONS: Joanne Brackeen, Benny Green, Horace Silver, Cedar Walton, James Williams

GEOFFREY KEEZER

CONVERSATIONS: Joanne Brackeen, Geoffrey Keezer, Mulgrew Miller, James Williams

PRINTED SOURCES:
Geoffrey Keezer: "He had an ability to open up your sound…"
 —Mike Hennessey, liner notes to *The Art of Jazz: Live at Leverkusen*, 1989

PIANO NOTES

CONVERSATIONS: Joanne Brackeen, Mulgrew Miller

PRINTED SOURCES:
John Hicks: "Art was pretty heavy on piano players…"
  —Joel Herson, *DownBeat*, June 1979
Art Blakey: "When I had Joanne Brackeen in the band…"
  —*Jazz Magazine*, winter 1979

CHAPTER 5
THE BIG BEAT: The Bass Clef

DOUG WATKINS

CONVERSATIONS: Charles Fambrough, Lonnie Plaxico

JYMIE MERRITT

CONVERSATIONS: Charles Fambrough, Lonnie Plaxico

CURTIS FULLER

CONVERSATIONS: Steve Davis, Geoffrey Keezer, Brian Lynch, Cedar Walton

REGGIE WORKMAN

CONVERSATIONS: Charles Fambrough, Lonnie Plaxico

DENNIS IRWIN

CONVERSATIONS: Charles Fambrough, Lonnie Plaxico, James Williams

CHARLES FAMBROUGH

CONVERSATIONS: Charles Fambrough, Branford Marsalis, Lonnie Plaxico, James Williams

LONNIE PLAXICO

CONVERSATIONS: Charles Fambrough, Lonnie Plaxico

ROBIN EUBANKS

CONVERSATIONS: Steve Davis, Robin Eubanks

PRINTED SOURCES:
Robin Eubanks: "Art was very instrumental in my development…"
  —Craig Jolley, *AllAboutJazz.com*, May 2001

STEVE DAVIS

CONVERSATIONS: Steve Davis, Robin Eubanks

ESSIET OKUN ESSIET

CONVERSATIONS: Charles Fambrough, Lonnie Plaxico

BASS CLEF NOTES

CONVERSATIONS: Steve Davis, Charles Fambrough, Donald Harrison, Lonnie
 Plaxico, James Williams

PRINTED SOURCES:
Frank Lacy: "The music of that era had a certain flow…"
 —Martin Johnson, *DownBeat*, November 1993

THEORY OF ART

CONVERSATIONS: Terence Blanchard, Joanne Brackeen, Donald Brown, Steve Davis,
 Benny Green, Freddie Hubbard, Javon Jackson, Brian Lynch, Chuck Mangione,
 Branford Marsalis, Wynton Marsalis, Mulgrew Miller, Valery Ponomarev, Horace
 Silver, Cedar Walton, Bobby Watson, James Williams

THE SIDEMEN OF ART BLAKEY AND THE JAZZ MESSENGERS

CONVERSATIONS: Terence Blanchard

PRINTED SOURCES:
The Art Blakey Chronology
 —Michael Fitzgerald and Steve Schwartz, 2001

Index

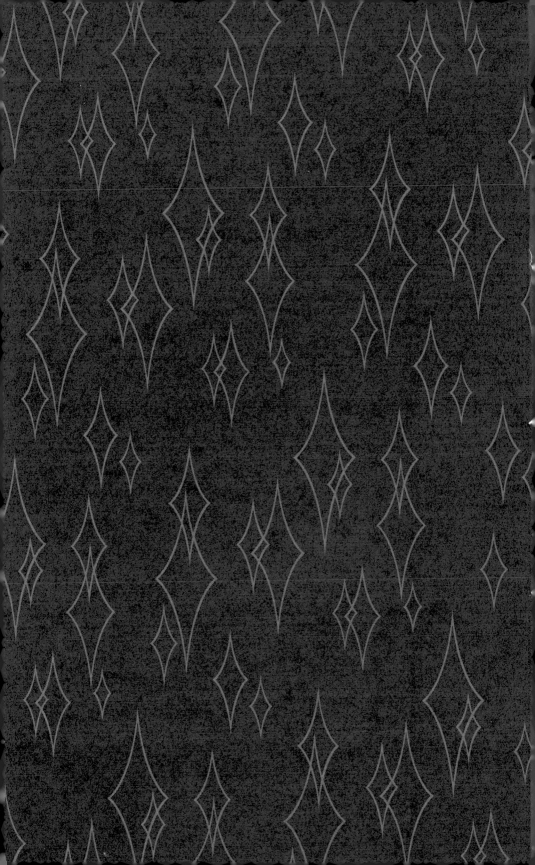